Endorsements

Dr. Andes, through her own personal experience and extensive research, has shown the light of truth into dark corners of our world, some seen, some unseen. She also dispels a lot of preconceived notions and long held beliefs that are just not true. Dr. Andes gives us Scripture to defeat the enemy on his own ground, where this is not being taught from our pulpits and in our churches today. This is an easy read and a must read for students, parents, and pastors alike.

—Fred Agey
Avid Book Critic-Culpeper, Virginia

This Scripturally based book gives insightful information explaining Satan's tactics and how one can recognize them. Dr. Andes clearly brings out what parents need to look for when their children get involved in the dark world. Anyone reading this book can use it as self-help to set themselves and others free of demonic influence.

—Rev. Leonard A. Preston MAT.
San Antonia, Texas

This is an excellent Bible primer to help set free those who are unaware of the oppression that comes from ungodly (occult and cult) practices. Dr. Andes' direction from the Holy Spirit during her long experience has helped make this a critically important book to every individual seeking to be free in Christ.

—Rev. Laurence V. Mason, Ph.D.
Pres. Agape Love Ministries, Inc.
Remington, Virginia

"My people are destroyed for lack of knowledge" (Hosea 4:6). Knowledge is powerful.

The information provided in this book is a must for every household.

—Rev. Suzanne Gregg MAT
Director of Life Christian University
Extension Campus. Amissville, Virginia

KNOW THY ENEMY

WHAT YOU DON'T KNOW CAN HURT YOU!

A practical guide to know and understand spiritual warfare and how to set the captives free.

By Donna Andes, Ph.D.

Xulon Press
10640 Main Street
Suite 204
Fairfax, VA 22030
(703) 934-4411
XulonPress.com

To order additional copies, call 1-866-909-BOOK (2665).

God Bless you!

Dr. Donna Ande

I wish to acknowledge all who helped me in

any way to write and rewrite this manuscript.

A special word of thanks to Alice Wolff, Pat Schaefer,

Elizabeth Wood, and Fred Agey.

*"Stand fast therefore in the liberty
by which Christ has made us free and
do not be entangled again with a yoke of bondage."*
Galatians 5:1 (NKJ).

THIS BOOK IS DEDICATED TO:

MY PRECIOUS LORD JESUS,

MY HELPER, THE HOLY SPIRIT,

MY SWEET HUSBAND WHO HAS

ALLOWED ME THE TIME TO WRITE,

AND ALL THOSE WHO WANT TO BE FREE.

Table of Contents

INTRODUCTION xv

PART 1 Satan

Chapter I
    The History and Origins of Satan............21

Chapter II
    The Methods and Functions of Satan.............25

Chapter III
    Satanic Influence Through Body,
    Soul and Spirit 29

Chapter IV
    Other Methods of Satanic Influence:
    Curses,Iniquities, Soul Ties,
    and Familiar Spirits...............................35

PART 2 Cults

Chapter V
    Definition of Cults and Occult 45

Chapter VI
    Traits Common to Cults 47

Chapter VII
Why People Enter Cults 53

PART 3 Names and Philosophies of Various Cults

Chapter VIII
Witchcraft, Cults, New Age:
Spiritism, Magic, Halloween, Gothic Movement,
UFO's, and Astrology...........................59

Chapter IX
Eastern Religions:
Yoga, Theosophy, Ananda Marga Yoga Society,
Hinduism, Buddhism, Taoism, and Islam 79

Chapter X
Western Religions:
Edgar Cayce (ARE), Free Masonry, Mormonism,
Unity Jehovah's Witness, and Unification.............95

PART 4 Holistic Medicine

Chapter XI
The Enemy's Tactics in Alternative Medicine:
Acupuncture, Iridology, Reiki, Ayurveda,
and Biofeedback 117

PART 5 Influences on Children and Youth

Chapter XII
Dangers of Fantasy Games:
Dungeon and Dragons, Pokemon,
Harry Potter Books, Magic Game,
Signs of Child Involvement 129

PART 6 Freedom from Cults and Attitudes Toward Cults

Chapter XIII
Discernment of Spirits, Set Free Through
Salvation, Filled With The Spirit,
Deliverance, Identification Form,
and Choose Blessings 139

PART 7 Christian's Responsibility for Aftercare

Chapter XIV 163

Introduction

There are so many people in spiritual bondage today. Even some Christians have not been set free. Jesus says to heal the sick, the lame, the blind and set the captives free as stated in Luke 4:18. Many people are not totally free of every type of curse, iniquity, or bondage, as God wants us to be. Understanding is needed to know where the bondage comes from. Some Christians believe that once we accept Jesus as our Lord and Savior; we are no longer under any curse. Jesus took the curse upon Himself (Galatians 3:13). His death on the cross, removed the curse placed upon us by the disobedience of Adam and Eve. This disobedience was the original sin that Jesus needed to redeem us from. However, if we persist in our sin and do what God told us not to do as listed in Deuteronomy 18:10-14, we are in disobedience and in bondage. The things mentioned in Deuteronomy are:

> "There shall not be found among you anyone who makes his son or his daughter pass through the fire, or one who practices witchcraft, or a soothsayer, or one who interprets omens, or a sorcerer, or one who conjures spells, or a medium, or a spiritist, or one who conjures up the dead. For all

who do these things are an abomination to the Lord, and because of these abominations the Lord your God drive them out from before you. You shall be blameless before the Lord your God. For these nations which you will dispossess listened to soothsayers and diviners; but as for you, the Lord your God has not appointed such for you."

Human beings are a tripartite being. This means that we have a body, soul, and spirit. In 1 Thessalonians 5:23 it says, "Now may the God of peace Himself sanctify you completely; and may your whole spirit, soul, and body; be preserved blameless at the coming of our Lord Jesus Christ." Sometimes our soul needs to be healed. This is the realm that evil spirits may set up camp (point of entry) or the emotions need healing from former traumatic experiences.

Any religion that does not believe in the deity of Christ, that He was born of a virgin, shed His blood by dying on a Cross for our sins, rose from the dead in three days, ascended into heaven, and sent us the Holy Spirit, is a cult. Exposure to the occult or cultic practices can influence our lives. The difference between the two terms will be explained. The main thrust of various cults will be explored in this book and the dangers of each. If we know about various cults and occult practices, we can better understand the people that have been involved. Basic cultic knowledge is essential for the one engaged in delivering someone from a cultic influence. There is helpful information how to become free without going through a deliverance with someone else doing the deliverance. After being set free, there are steps one can take to remain free. When a person is released from bondage of a cult, support and encouragement, done patiently with love is necessary or they may revert back to their previous cultic environment. The purpose of this book is to inform people of the knowledge of the enemy, how to become free from the enemies bondages and to remain free.

The enemy is out to attack our children. I have met many women who have survived an abortion attack by their mother while they were still in the womb. This opened the child up to abandonment and the spirit of rejection. Satan's tactic would be to kill babies before they were born so they could not do damage to his kingdom here on earth. He goes about seeking whom he can devour (1 Peter 5:8).

Children can be filled with fear and violent actions through the influence of television. Years ago when I was studying psychology in nursing, I learned that what we put into our minds today, we will become in five years. We can see children's behavior being lived out today by their environment and through what they watch on television. There is violence, immoral sexual behavior and witchcraft being experienced and can be later demonstrated in the lives of our children. Certain violent, destructive or evil games, toys, cartoons, movies, and computer games also influence our young people. Adults can be informed what to watch for when a child begins to manifest different behavior.

Many people today are looking for alternative medical treatment. It is estimated about 300 people a day in the United States die from legitimate prescription drugs. Because of that, people want to know which alternative therapies are acceptable without being exposed to the dark world of Satan. The philosophy of a few of them will be covered and how to discern which treatments are safe.

Too few people know how to set the captives free. There is an attempt to share information from personal experiences and from those who are in a deliverance ministry, on how to set those in bondage free. After being set free, one then needs to be taught how to stay free. This is best accomplished through salvation, being empowered by the Holy Spirit, and the Word of God. Jesus is the way, the truth, and the life (John 14:6). We have a responsibility not only to set the captives free but also carry the responsibility as a Christians to help a person remain free from demonic activity in order to prevent them from returning to their old way of living.

PART 1

Satan

Chapter I

The History And Origins Of Satan

Knowledge of our enemy, is what everyone ought to know. Our spiritual enemy is Satan, an adversary who goes about, seeking who he can devour (1 Peter 5:8). We know Satan was in the Garden of Eden at the time Adam and Eve were tempted. He deceived Adam and Eve, and he is still in the deceiving business and is our enemy.

We need to be concerned about Satan. Let me explain where he came from. In Ezekiel it tells us that he was before the throne of God, he was a cherub, what he looked like and what he did. It states in Ezekiel 28:12-20:

> "Son of man, take up a lamentation for the king of Tyre, and say to him, 'Thus says the Lord God: You were the seal of perfection, full of wisdom and perfect in beauty. You were in Eden, the garden of God; every precious stone was your covering: The sardius, topaz, and diamond, beryl, onyx,

and jasper, sapphire, turquoise, and emerald with gold. The workmanship of your timbrels and pipes was prepared for you on the day you were created. You were the anointed cherub who covers; I established you; you were on the holy mountain of God; you walked back and forth in the midst of fiery stones. You were perfect in your ways from the day you were created, till iniquity was found in you. By the abundance of your trading you became filled with violence within, and you sinned; therefore I cast you as a profane thing out of the mountain of God; and I destroyed you, O covering cherub, from the midst of the fiery stones. Your heart was lifted up because of your beauty; you corrupted your wisdom for the sake of your splendor; I cast you to the ground, I laid you before kings, that they might gaze at you.' "

Satan was filled with pride and desired equality with the Lord. Satan's statement is recorded in Isaiah 14:14, "I will ascend above the heights of the clouds, I will be like the Most High." After this boast God speaks to Satan in Ezekiel 28:17, and casts him to the earth. We see that he indeed goes about the world seeking whom he can devour. Satan is the ruler of this world (John 12:31).

From Ezekiel 28:13 we realize the concept that not only was he beautiful, but he had musical abilities as well. Satan apparently was a superb choir director or at least a praiser before God's throne. We know there were angels around the throne of God, as in Revelation 4:8, they continually say, "Holy, holy, holy." It is likely that Satan was one of those angelic beings worshipping God around His throne.

Satan knew music very well. This is probably the reason he can entice a nation or culture by the type of music he instills. Rock music is a good example of his influence.

It has been reported that at rock concerts some people, mostly young people, will take vows to serve Satan. Once people take this step, they can be in a downward spiral being used as puppets for Satan's kingdom. They must be rescued from his clutches before it is too late. Satan indeed is the god of this world. He comes to cheat, kill and to destroy. Jesus came so that they might have life and have it more abundantly (John 10:10).

When death entered the universe as a result of Adam and Eve's sin; death also came to man. Satan is prince of the power of the air and works in the sons of disobedience (Ephesians 2:2). Jesus died on the cross to redeem us from sin. "Then comes the end, when He delivers the kingdom to God the Father, when He puts an end to all rule and all authority and power." (1 Corinthians 15:24). Satan's time here on earth is getting shorter.

In the same chapter verses 33 and 34 God says, "Do not be deceived: 'Evil company corrupts good habits.' Awake to righteousness, and do not sin; for some do not have the knowledge of God. I speak this to your shame." It is essential to know God's word, have knowledge of Satan's tactics, and avoid all demonic or cultic contacts as well as avoidance of anything that involves the occult. God's word very clearly states our close friends are not to be evil people. "You cannot drink the cup of the Lord and the cup of demons; you cannot partake of the Lord's table and of the table of demons" (1 Corinthians 10:21). Sin in our lives gives Satan the right of entry into our being.[1]

Chapter II

The Methods And Functions Of Satan

Howard O. Pittman explains the function of demons in his book, *Demons An Eyewitness Account*, written after he had a near death experience. His experience began as six doctors were trying to save his life in the Emergency Room. Each breath taken by Mr. Pittman was sheer will power. He is a Christian and called on God to permit him to appear before the throne of God to plead for an extension of his life. He heard no voice but experienced great peace. Then he heard a voice saying, "Stop! Do not breathe. It will all be over. All you ever would want will be yours." Thinking the voice was God's, he tried to stop breathing, and like a bolt of lightening, he remembered asking God for an extension of his life. He realized the voice was from Satan! He resisted and Satan fled from Mr. Pittman.

Knowing Satan's tactics of adding some truth to his lies, Mr. Pittman realized Satan's deception by promising him no pain. Satan then promised that Mr. Pittman could have all he ever wanted if he would obey and stop breathing. The scripture records several examples of Satan's work on believers as quoted by Howard Pittman:

> "He uses wiles (2 Corinthians 2:11), and that he afflicts believers (Luke 13:16). Satan insinuates or implies doubt (Genesis 3:1), that he misuses scripture (Matthew 4:1-11). We see also that he is the accuser of good men (Job 1:8-10), that he resists good men (Zechariah 3:1-3), and that he tempts men to sin (1 Chronicles 21:1), We know that he has the ability to blind the mind of man so that man may not believe the very gospel of Christ (2 Corinthians 4:4)" (Pittman: 9).

He was before God in heaven and God instructed Mr. Pittman to go back to earth and told him He wanted him to tell the people on earth how Satan and his cohorts operated. In giving Mr. Pittman these instructions, God allowed him to visit what Mr. Pittman called second heaven, the domain of demons. An angel escorted Mr. Pittman's spirit through a dimensional wall; and he felt the special permission and protection of the Holy Spirit.

In the second heaven he saw Satan's social order, which was discriminatory and it was set up like the caste system in India. The caste system produced "untouchables" in the second heaven like it does on earth.

As he traveled through the second heaven, he discovered each demon is an expert in his field. There was no love at all, none for their master or for themselves. We can see this in operation today on earth with two people that are arguing, fighting, or even killing each other. We do not fight flesh and blood (Ephesians 6:12).

The escorting angel pointed out each demonic group. The demons were all sizes and shapes. Some looked like humans (even giant humans), some half man and half animal. Others looked like our animals but were just horrible in appearance. Some forms of demons were so grotesque, the mind could not imagine (Revelation16:13).

The highest echelon was the warring demons. This group supplies all princes as well as formulates the plans to create wars and rumors of wars upon the earth. They were proud, beautiful, strong, powerful, cunning, intelligent, and looked like men in a Roman armor. Wickedness in high places was their assignment.

The next echelon were demons of greed. These demons were well dressed like businessmen in suits. Their assignment was to destroy the economies of the world. They operate worldwide by spirits of hate, lust, strife, and power hungry spirits.

The third ranking order of demons were those who possessed skills in the area of dark arts such as witchcraft, false religions, meditation, self destruction, fear, magic, sorcery, hypnosis, occult worship, ESP, psychedelic drugs, other psychic phenomena, necromancy (speaking with the dead), and anything else that involves the mind. The demons appeared to be part man and part animal like the figures in Greek mythology.

The next group was called the mystery demons. They are required to ask special permission from God to work on certain individuals. They can work on children also. Mr. Pittman says, "Over ninety percent of all demonic activity in humans is at or over the level of accountability. It is done so on a permission basis only." He also believes epilepsy is one of their manifestations as well as great power over a persons flesh because of its anonymity (Pittman: 19).

The last group of demons was so horrible to look at. They had despicable shapes and sizes. Moral perversion was their assignment. Howard Pittman said if people could see these demons, they would never enjoy perversion again!

Chapter III

Satanic Influence Through Body, Soul and Spirit

There are various ways a demonic spirit can influence a person. We know from the Word of God that we are a tripartite person. God tells us in 1 Thessalonians 5:23, "Now may the God of peace Himself sanctify you completely; and may your whole spirit, soul, and body be preserved blameless at the coming of our Lord Jesus Christ." From this scripture we know we are body, soul and spirit.

When a person becomes saved, Jesus comes into that human spirit and it is regenerated. This is confirmed in John 3:6 where it says, "That which is born of the flesh is flesh, and that which is born of the Spirit is spirit." One's spirit is filled with God and it is full of Jesus. No darkness can reside with light. No demon can possess a Christian. Demons can only attack through the body or soul of a born again believer. We know the enemy can attack the body because a Christian can become physically ill. A spirit of infirmity attacks the person. Acts 10:38 states, that Jesus healed all that were oppressed by the devil.

Consider the soul of man. Our soul is our mind, intellect, will, emotions, and conscience. Our soul according to Webster is a person's total self. Our intellect is the power to know things, to learn, ability to comprehend and our intelligence. Can we see a thought? Our minds can think good, kind, fair, loving thoughts or bad, judgmental, unforgiving, angry, impure, and evil thoughts. Paul says to have the mind of Christ (1 Corinthians 2:16). Demons can only attack the body or soul.

Sometimes there is a war going on in a person. This is made clear in Galatians 5:16-17 where it says, "I say then: Walk in the Spirit, and you shall not fulfill the lust of the flesh. For the flesh lusts against the Spirit, and the Spirit against the flesh; and these are contrary to one another, so that you do not do the things that you wish." Choices are made by the will.

The soul then thinks about a thing such as sin. It decides through the will. The flesh through the five senses of the body brings the desire to the mind, (soul) and the will makes the decision. The decision not to sin is made according to a correct conscience that has been formed by the Holy Spirit. We know there is conflict from the words of Romans 8:7-8 as it says, "Because the carnal mind is enmity against God; for it is not subject to the law of God, nor indeed can be, so then, those who are in the flesh cannot please God." When man's soul is out of proper relationship with his spirit it is contrary to God's highest will.

Here is an example to show the relationship between the soul, body, and spirit by a well-known person with a deliverance ministry. He was delivering "Cindy" of demons, who had three personalities. One personality was Cindy, one Karen, and one Barbara (fictitious names). She had been to many places for therapy and on many drugs, but she still had multiple personalities. By the time she called the ministry she had already accepted Jesus as Lord of her life.

Usually when the demonic spirits are commanded to leave, they would go; just like they did when Jesus rebuked them. This had been done to Cindy before, but the demons were still there. An explanation is that Jesus knew everything about Satan and his cohorts and they had to leave. We do not know everything, as we are not God. The person in charge of the deliverance would ask the demon its name and what right it had to be there. It spoke through Cindy and said, "Perversion when she was conceived." Then perversion was cast out through the power, blood and name of Jesus.

The personality of Karen came when she was nine years old. Her drunken father was beating down the door to come into her room. She was hiding in the closet. This spirit said it came to her in the name of Karen to protect her. This was when she took on that spirit along with the spirit of fear. There was a similar situation for her third personality.

After she was delivered, the one delivering her made her speak to each personality to be one with Cindy, her real name. She had to speak to her spirit, soul, and body to be one in Christ. She was completely delivered of multiple personalities. This exemplifies the necessary unity in a person as a tripartite being.

As human beings, since we possess a body, soul and spirit as stated in 1 Thessalonians 5:23, our spirit is a human spirit. It is explained in 1 Corinthians 15: 44-46 where it says, "It is sown a natural body, it is raised a spiritual body. There is a natural body, and there is a spiritual body. And so it is written, 'The first man Adam became a living being'. The last Adam became a life-giving spirit. However, the spiritual is not first, but the natural, and afterward the spiritual." At salvation Jesus comes into our spirit and it is regenerated. If we do not listen to the Holy Spirit, we operate out of our human spirit. Prayers can become soulish and we would be leaning to our own understanding.

Here is another example of how the body, soul, and spirit operate. Dr. Rebecca Brown was a medical doctor specializing in oncology. The Lord told her she could continue doing oncology and serve Him, or go into a deliverance ministry. He promised to show her every step of the way so she could set the captives free. She chose to go all the way with the Lord.

In her book, *He Came To Set The Captives Free*, Dr. Brown tells about a Satanic high priestess named Elaine. God impressed upon her that she was going to use her to set Elaine free. She explains how spirit bodies are under the control of an unsaved soul. She states: "Satan's goal is to teach humans to again regain the conscious control of their spiritual bodies and many do. Once this is achieved, these people can perceive the spirit world as well as the physical world. They can talk freely with demons; leave their physical bodies with their spirit bodies, and what seems to the average human, supernatural power. It was with their spirit bodies that the various witches and warlocks, without being physically present, would pull Elaine and myself out of bed, throw us across the room, etc. We were unable to see them because our physical eyes cannot see the spirit world. God does not want His people to control their spirit bodies in such a manner. If we did so, not only would we be open to overwhelming temptations to sin, we would not need to be dependent upon Him and we would also be constantly aware of Satan and his kingdom" (p.169).

Dr. Brown goes on to explain the imagination is the link between the soul and the spirit. This is what happens when people play the Ouija Board, Dungeon and Dragons, and other role-playing fantasy games. This is why the Word says to bring every thought into the captivity of Christ (2 Corinthians 10:3). When people are being delivered from the soulish power, those delivering must ask the Lord to remove the ability to perceive the spirit world. The one doing the deliverance must ask the Lord to sever all ties between the soul and spirit of the one being delivered. This is verified in Hebrews 4:12 where it says "For the Word of God is living and powerful, and sharper than any two-edged sword, piercing even to the division of soul and spirit, and of joints and marrow, and is a discerner of the thoughts and intents of the heart." Speaking God's living Word will heal and bring life to the person. James 4:2 says, "You lust and do not have. You murder and covet and cannot obtain. You fight and war. Yet you do not have because you do not ask." All we have to do is ask and we shall receive. God says in John 15:7, "If you abide in Me, and My words abide in you, you will ask what you desire, and it shall be done for you." It is so simple that it seems hard.

Chapter IV

Other Methods of Satanic Influence

E xodus 20:5 says, "You shall not bow down to them nor serve them. For I, the LORD your God, am a jealous God, visiting the iniquities of the fathers upon the children to the third and fourth generations of those who hate Me." A generation according to the dictionary is about thirty years. We do not know what unrepented sin our ancestors died with one hundred and twenty years ago. The results of these sins come down the bloodline and are called curses. In the physical realm the doctors call it hereditary. In the spirit realm they are considered curses.

Another definition of a curse by Webster is that it is evil that comes as if in response to imprecation or as retribution (p. 204). The unrepented sin is imprecated sin on ones fore-fathers and comes down the bloodline. How many times have we heard, "He's just like his father, or his grandfather did it too, or she's the black sheep in the family." Such traits are coming down the family line.

Jesus was prophesied in the Book of Isaiah 53:5 where it says, "But He was wounded for our transgressions, He was bruised for our iniquities; the chastisement for our peace was upon Him, and by His stripes we are healed." When Jesus was wounded for our transgressions, that was like a cut or break in the skin. When they used a whip with tips, it cut the flesh causing a wound. *Vines Expository Dictionary of New Testament Words* defines wound "trauma," as a blow, a stroke or smitten (p. 238).

Jesus was wounded for our transgressions. According to *Vines*, transgression (parabates) means to overstep the limits, primarily aside like a breach of the law. In other words disobeying God's commandments is called this breach, namely; sin (p.150).

He was bruised for our iniquities. Iniquities in *Vines* are "onomia," meaning lawlessness or wickedness. It literally means unrighteousness (p.260). Webster defines "iniquities" as a gross injustice or wickedness, or a violation of right or duty, wicked act, or sin (p.492). On the other hand, *Strong's Exhaustive Concordance* says that iniquity in the Book of Isaiah is " avown," meaning a moral evil, fault, iniquity, mischief, punishment (of iniquity) or sin (p. 86). From this we can conclude that iniquities are the result of, or punishment for sin. Iniquities appear to go deeper into the soul of a person. If there is no repentance by the person that sinned, the iniquities also come down the bloodline.

When I worked in the Emergency Room at the hospital, many times accident victims were brought in. Sometimes they would have superficial wounds and other times they would have just a scratch and no external injuries. Often there was deep internal bruising, even ruptured organs with internal bleeding. This bruising was not visible to the naked eye, but was deep within. The next day they would have many black and blue bruise marks and possibly black eyes from internal hemorrhaging. Iniquities can be deeply hidden within one's subconscious like a bruise.

Iniquities are not visible externally but the results of them can be seen. An example would be Abram and Sarai before their names were changed. God promised them an offspring. He said they would have as many offspring as there are stars in the sky and grains of sand on the seashore. They were impatient and got ahead of God.

Sarai asked Abram to sleep with her maidservant Hagar. Abram did and Hagar conceived Ishmael (Genesis 16:4). The descendants of Ishmael are visible today. Many of the Moslem people in the Middle East are Ishmael's offspring. Even though Abram repented of his sin, the iniquities or results of Abram's sin are still present today.

Another example may be a young girl that is overcome by a lustful boy. They commit the sin of fornication. They can repent for their sin but if she got pregnant; she still needs to bear the child. Someday that child may have children. The iniquity of fornication can come down the bloodline.

It is also possible the girl received a spirit of lust from the boy. This spirit could cause her to seduce other boys and she picks up their bad spirits as well. Next thing we know she can be called a "whore" or be into prostitution. Her life can go from bad to worse. It does not have to but often times it does. This can lead to drinking, drugs, crime, and involvement in cults. People like her are looking to fill the emptiness, guilt, and shame they feel. Only Jesus can fill this void and remove the guilt.

Having a sexual relationship outside of marriage causes problems. Not only can spirits be transferred as was the case with the first example I gave, but also "soul ties" are formed. In 1 Corinthians 6:15-16 it says, "Do you not know that your bodies are members of Christ? Shall I then take the members of Christ and make them members of a harlot? Certainly not! Or do you not know that he who is joined to a harlot is one body with her? For 'the two' He says, 'Shall become

37

one flesh.' But he who is joined to the Lord is one spirit with Him." Once soul ties are formed, they can be broken through the power, blood and name of Jesus. God's will is that soul ties would not be made with anyone who is not their lawful marriage partner in the first place.

When we confess the curses coming down the bloodline from generations, we also need to confess the iniquities of the generational sins. We may have someone bind the curses (Matthew 18:18) and the iniquities off us as we verbally confess our sins. Jesus will remove and break all soul ties through the power in His name (Philippians 2:10).

Pastor Larry Huck was teaching on Trinity Broadcasting Network and giving his testimony. He had been an alcoholic and drug addict. After he got saved he was led to go into the ministry. Following seminary he became a very successful Pastor of a large church. One day in rage he threw his son against the wall. He said he was just like his father who also had fits of rage! He could not preach one thing and do another.

As he sought the Lord, God began to reveal to him from 1 Peter 2:24 and Isaiah 53:5, that he could have victory. He was delivered not only from the generational curses but also from the iniquities of those curses. He explained that many Christians are Christians all their life and still do not have victory over a particular sin or fault. They need to be delivered from the iniquities as well. Ancestral sins could be divorce, adultery, fornication, incest, homosexuality, anger, rage, alcohol, drugs, stealing, lying, gambling, and the lists go on. There is hope and help through Jesus who desires to set the captives free.

Some people may argue that Jesus bore the curse for us, and wonder how they could still have a bad habit. They wonder if they are saved, with Jesus in their heart, how could this be? They lived for Him and yet do not have the victory over sin.

When a balloon is filled with helium, can we see the helium? All we know is that if we let the balloon go, it will rise up and is carried away. We see the results of it, not the air that did it. To compare, we cannot see the iniquities, but the results of them.

Another way that Satan can have a hold on ones life is from former involvement in a cult. This is another example from *He Came To Set The Captives Free* by Dr. Rebecca Brown. The Lord directed her to take Elaine into her home. Elaine had taken on many demons over a seventeen-year period. Satan was trying to attack them both. There was bound to be double trouble! Both prayed and rebuked Satan, covered themselves with the blood of Jesus and did all they knew to do.

For weeks they could not sleep as things were flying around the room and they were being bounced out of their beds. Dr. Brown cried out to God for an answer. He quickened the scripture in Exodus 40:9 which says, "And you shall take the anointing oil, and anoint the tabernacle and all that is in it; and you shall hallow it and all its utensils, and it shall be holy." Immediately she anointed her home, all objects in her home and both of them. After everything was anointed holy and sacred as unto the Lord, all the astral projection stopped. There was peace. The Holy Spirit placed a hedge of protection around them.

Elaine was gradually delivered from the demons she had acquired while becoming powerful in Satan's kingdom. It is believed that demons cannot read our minds, but they can put many ideas in ones mind. The demons are not omnipresent like God for they can only be in one place at a time. There continued to be an unseen spiritual drawing of demonic spirits to Elaine until she was completely delivered. All cultic involvement must be renounced in the name of Jesus.

A twelve year-old girl, who was a distant relative of

mine, got involved in Satanism at school. She tried to shoot her father, but fortunately she missed. Her uncle was a Sheriff's Deputy and said this incident needed to be reported, which they did. During the investigation they found rock music tapes, satanic jewelry, recipes of spells and other witchcraft items in her bedroom. Her diary and book of spells were given to her aunt. One day while my husband and I were visiting her aunt, she gave us the tablet of witches' spells. Being curious, I looked down on the page of spells for healing and a cold eerie force came at me. I threw the tablet down and covered all of us with the blood of Jesus. I asked her to dispose of all the items she had received from her niece and explained that demons can attach themselves to these objects and continue to influence them. They can affect our health, finances, our minds, personal relationships and all things pertaining to our lives and loved ones.

The girl was sent to a juvenile detention center and was assigned a Christian psychologist. He had our prayer group praying for her salvation. God answered our prayers and she gave her heart to Jesus. That was the first step. Her parents put her in a Christian School were she made new friends, became involved in a Christian Youth Group, and continued with her out patient therapy. It was important that the therapist be a Christian, as the therapist understands that one cannot treat the body and soul like secular psychologists do. We are a tripartite being made into His image. The soul part needs to be renewed through the Word of God and by His Spirit. All things can become new just like it says in 2 Corinthians 5:17, "Therefore, if anyone is in Christ, he is a new creation; old things have passed away; behold, all things have become new." This young lady is now living a peaceful Christian life and is doing very well.

SATANIC INFLUENCE THROUGH FAMILIAR SPIRITS

Familiar spirits can come from any rank of demons. An example was King Saul when he contacted the witch of Endor. Saul requested that she conjure up the spirit of the dead. When she did what Saul requested, Samuel appeared (1 Samuel 28). We learn from Deuteronomy 18:9-12 that necromancy is an abomination unto the Lord. Webster defines necromancy as conjuration of the spirits of the dead for purposes of magical revealing the future or influencing the course of events (p. 565). Sometimes after the death of a loved one, a living relative may begin to talk to the deceased. This of course aught to be discouraged.

Mary Garrison in her book, *How To Try A Spirit*, classifies the spirit of divination along with a familiar spirit. She lists these as other manifestations of the spirits: Diviner (water witching), Soothsayers (observer of times, horoscopes, almanacs), Enchanters (magicians), Witches or Wizard (those who practice witchcraft and sorcery), Hypnotist (a charmer), Clairvoyant people, Necromancy (one who consults the dead), Star Gazers (one who studies and worships the stars), Astrologers (those used in an effort to foretell the future), Belomancy (divination by arrows), splanchonmancy (divination by inspection of entrails), Teraphim (images consulted for advice), Mutterers (one who communicates with a familiar spirit as if talking to himself), Ventriloquist (a person who throws their voice), Peeping Toms (who get sexual fulfillment from watching others from a concealed place), Mimicry or Pantomime's could also manifest a familiar spirit (p.41-42). In addition to this I would like to add augury (interpretation of signs or omens), psychometrics (identifying characteristics of a person through some object he wore or used), telchenesis (moving objects without tangible cause), apparitions and soul travel. These are not a complete list but are the essential ones.

Those with a familiar spirit have a "spirit guide" who one talks to or it gives them direction. It can be a very friendly close companion. This is often the case with children and with many of their friends. The demons purpose is to entice people away from God.

One time I was responsible for the kindergarten worship service. I asked them (about ten children), if they had an imaginary playmate. They all raised their hands. I then asked how many talked to them. One little boy's hand went up and said he had lots of them at Grandpa's. (I knew Grandpa was an alcoholic). I explained that the only one we need to talk to is Jesus. Under my breath I bound a deceptive spirit in Jesus name. Then he asked if the Bible said he was not to talk to them. When I replied "yes," he quickly said he would not do it any more. Today he is a fine young man who appears to love the Lord.

Another example of a familiar spirit is when I was teaching fourth graders at Sunday School. I noticed one girl had a difficult time being tuned in to the things of the Spirit. She was there because she had to be. The Spirit prompted me to ask if any of the children had imaginary friends or playmates when they were younger. This girl raised her hand and said she still did and still talked with them! I explained it was a demon and we can talk with Jesus or the Holy Spirit just as well. She apparently took it to heart and stopped the practice. She is a changed girl when it comes to spiritual things. I prayed with her when it was appropriate and took authority over it in Jesus name. Like it says in Luke 4:18, "The Spirit of the LORD is upon Me, because He has anointed Me to preach the gospel to the poor; He has sent Me to heal the brokenhearted, to proclaim liberty to the captives and recovery of sight to the blind, to set at liberty those who are oppressed; to proclaim the acceptable year of the LORD." Today she is sweet loving girl and is a successful student in a Christian school.

PART 2

Cults

Chapter V

Definition of Cults and Occult

For one to understand cults, one has to know what a cult is. Webster's Dictionary defines a cult as:

1. A small and particular system of religious worship, especially with reference to its rites and ceremonies.
2. A group that devotes itself to or venerates a person, ideal etc.
3. A religion or sect considered to be false, unorthodox, or extremist (p.233).

It can also mean, pertaining to any system claiming use or knowledge of secret or super natural powers or agencies, beyond ordinary knowledge or understanding. We often hear the word occult and can get confused. Webster defines occult as: secret, disclosed or communicated only to the initiated (p.583). The term cult applies to the type of group and occult refers to the characteristics or paraphernalia of a group.

The importance or significance of knowing about cults is because God says, "My people are destroyed for lack of knowledge." (Hosea 4:6). For us to be more than conquerors in the Lord we need to understand whom our enemy is. By not knowing our enemy, it gives him the opportunity to pursue and conquer us without being aware of it. By our knowledge, God may use us to set the captives free and to discern a false prophet.

We know how Satan functions from the Word of God. In Ephesians 6:12, it tells us there are powers, principalities, spirits of darkness, and those that are in high places. We know there is a hierarchy of demonic forces and also from 1 Peter 3:22 where it says, "who has gone into heaven and is at the right hand of God, angels and authorities and powers having been made subject to Him." This fits the picture of what Howard Pittman saw when he visited the second heaven.

The word principalities according to *Vines*, comes from the Greek word *arche,* meaning beginnings. It means the first rule. It signifies not the first estate of fallen angels, but their authoritative power, "Their own" indicating that which had been assigned to them by God, which they left, aspiring to prohibited conditions (p. 213). The word ruler, *archon* is a chief, a prince or a ruler. It is not against flesh and blood, but spiritual rulers in the world. They are world rulers of darkness (p. 307).

It is Satan and his cohorts that roam around seeking who they can devour. It is up to us to keep our guard up and to not fall prey to his tactics. In 1 John 3:8 it says, "He who sins is of the devil, for the devil has sinned from the beginning. For this purpose the Son of God was manifested, that He might destroy the works of the devil." When we fall prey to sin, we can get up quickly because of Jesus.

Chapter VI

Traits Common to Cults

There are several traits or characteristics that are common to all cults. They are enlightenment, reincarnation, and meditation. There are traits that describe specific cults but these three are inherent to most of them. Enlighten comes from the word "photizo," which simply signifies to give light, shine, to enlighten, illumine (*Vines*: 31). In cultic thinking enlightenment means to negate reality. To people who think they are enlightened, logic plays no part in it. The so-called enlightened ones try to blank out their mind and it opens their minds to satanic infiltration.

Buddha himself is an example of enlightenment. He wandered around outside of his home compound for six years. When he sat under a *Pipal Bodhi* (wisdom) tree, he claimed to have a heightened awareness experience. In fact the name of Buddha means "enlightened one." The cult history goes back to 600 B.C. Even today people are still seeking enlightenment.

Bob Larson writes in his book, *Larson's New Book Of Cults*, that Buddha summarized his discovery of enlightenment in three premises: 1.) existence in suffering, 2.) desire causes suffering, 3.) ridding all desire ends suffering. These precepts led to a fourth conclusion: desire can be eradicated by following Buddha's Eightfold Path (a sacred path with eight branches that leads someone who desires to be delivered from suffering). Eightfold Path is defined as a right belief, (correctly understanding his "Four Noble Truths" without superstition), right speech (speaking truthfully), right resolve (keeping pure motives), right conduct (living peacefully and honestly), right livelihood (choosing a job that does not harm others), right thought (keeping an active self critical mind), right effort (seeking knowledge with self control), right concentration (zealously practicing meditation and Raja Yoga).

Since the Eightfold Path of spiritual insights became known as the Four Noble Truths, this is considered to be a so-called middle way between Atticism (a characteristic feature of attic Greek language or Literature) and Hedonism (a doctrine that pleasure or happiness is the sole or chief good in life) (Larson p. 73). It is hard to visualize how his theory on suffering can enlighten anyone.

Mystics seek enlightenment. Webster defines a mystic as mystical, which means having a spiritual meaning or reality that is neither apparent to the senses nor obvious to the intelligence. He also describes it as relating to, or resulting from an individual's direct communion with God or ultimate reality (p.560). Most mystics believe enlightenment is from God. If the revelation lacks truth of God's Word, then it is from the god of this world. Christian mystics will acknowledge Jesus and the Holy Spirit for their enlightenment. Webster tells us that mystics or mystical experiences can result from an individual's direct communion with God or an ultimate reality (p.560). One must be very careful to discern which entity it is.

The Hindu religion, which is the common religion of

India, has another concept of enlightenment. It is based upon the religion of the original Aryan settlers as they expounded and evolved in the Vedas, Upanishads, Bagavad-Gito, etc. (Webster: p. 450). The Hindus believe the highest form of enlightenment is when nothingness is reached. The Hindus call this nothingness a "force" or Brahma.

Brahmin is a member of the highest, or priestly, class among the Hindus. They reach this state of Brahma by not believing in a personal God. Believing there is no personal God there is no one to be responsible to; therefore there is no sin. The more they try to get into the truth the more they realize there is no truth. They are deceived and cannot find truth outside of Jesus (John 14;6).

Satan influences the so-called "enlightened" ones. He goes about the world seeking whom he may devour. He comes like a thief to steal, to kill, and destroy (John 10:10). He also transforms himself as an angel of light. In 2 Corinthians 11:15 it says, "Therefore it is no great thing if his ministers also transform themselves into ministers of righteousness, whose end will be according to their works." We can know the ones enlightened by the fruits of their life. The lives of the "enlightened ones" do not line up with the Word of God. Because of this, it indicates that it is a cult.

Reincarnation is the second common trait of cults. Webster defined reincarnation as the belief the soul, upon death of the body comes back to earth in another body or form or a rebirth of the soul in a new body (p.793). The word incarnate means to be given a bodily or human form. The "re" means to do it again. So those who believe in reincarnation think that when they die their souls go back to nothingness. It then can come back into someone or something other than who they were.

Those who believe in reincarnation also believe there are levels of beings they can return to inhabit. What ever they are in this life they will come back in a higher level. For example there is much suffering in this life, the next life will be better because they did their suffering in this life. This is their "karma." In Hinduism and Buddhism the "karma" is seen as bringing upon oneself inevitable results, either in this life or in a reincarnation (Webster p. 523). It is as if their past will determine their future.

The Buddhists and Hindus in India will throw a newborn child into the trash or river if they think it has a bad "karma." They will not kill a cow or a rat because it is sacred. It may be a former relative. Even the cows urine and dung is considered holy for the same reason. Reincarnation fulfills the laws of "karma" for them.

People who have guilt will easily believe in reincarnation so they can live their lives over in another life. They think they can straighten out their lives if they have another chance. Perhaps they might even be elevated into a higher level. They are now paying for what they did in the past. They believe if they mess up in each life, they get what they deserved.

Christians do not need to believe in reincarnation. Romans 6:4,8,9 states, "Therefore we were buried with Him through baptism into death, that just as Christ was raised from the dead by the glory of the Father, even so we also should walk in newness of life. Now if we died with Christ, we believe that we shall also live with Him, knowing that Christ, having been raised from the dead, dies no more. Death no longer has dominion over Him." This Scriptures states that when we die our souls go to be with Christ and not into another person. The Old Testament clearly states in Ecclesiastes 12:7, "Then the dust will return to the earth as it was, and the spirit will return to God who gave it." The New Testament says our suffering should be for the sake of Christ and not the reincarnated belief that if we suffer here now there will be less suffering in the next life. It is clear in Philippians 1:21,29, "For to me, to live is

Christ, and to die is gain . . . For to you it has been granted on behalf of Christ, not only to believe in Him, but also to suffer for His sake." Christians can rejoice knowing their next life is with God.

Meditation is the third trait of cults. According to *Webster's Dictionary* meditation is defined: to disengage in thought, to contemplate or reflect (p.594). The meditation of cults is to disengage oneself from reality or environment. The ones meditating are to shut off their feelings. The mind and will is considered an enemy and therefore is to have no input into them. Meditation of the cults is achieved by chanting (repetitive mantra), jumping, breathing a certain way, sitting long periods in a "lotus" position, staring at a blank wall, by fasting, and mind altering drugs. The mind is then open to anything that comes to it. The one meditating becomes mentally disassociated. This type of cultic meditation is to bring peace and cause them not to worry about the things of the world. Cults empty their minds whereas Christians meditate on Godly things in an attempt to reach a closer walk with God. Cults are emptying out their minds and Christians are being filled up with the peace and joy of the Lord. God tells us in His Word to meditate on it and consider what has been written. Listen to what God says in Psalm 119:11-16, "How can a young man cleanse his way? By taking heed according to Your word. With my whole heart I have sought You; oh, let me not wander from Your commandments! Your word I have hidden in my heart, that I might not sin against You. Blessed are You, O LORD! Teach me Your statutes. With my lips I have declared all the judgments of Your mouth. I have rejoiced in the way of Your testimonies, as much as in all riches. I will meditate on Your precepts, and contemplate Your ways. I will delight myself in Your statutes; I will not forget Your word."

Christians view life from a horizontal perspective of

past, present and future. Cults view it from a vertical perspective, which they believe is a higher elevation. Christians believe in Christ's resurrection where as Cults believe in reincarnation. There is a vast difference between the two like the difference between light and darkness.

Chapter VII

Why People Enter Cults

One cannot help wonder why any one would want to enter a cult. Many people enter cults because of deep guilt. They are attracted to the concept of reincarnation so they can have another chance in their next life. Usually they are lonely or in despair. The cult group extends attention and affection at first to ensnare them and as a result they enter because of feelings rather than doctrine. Cults can fulfill an emotional need that many people have.

People who need a sense of belonging and acceptance and have not received it elsewhere are also drawn to cults. This meaningful sense of belonging allows them to accept the domineering authority of cult members. Sometimes it goes so far they begin to believe the founder of a cult is God. It is not uncommon to find some founders actually believe they are God. They even expect their followers to worship them.

While meditating on nothing or staring at a spot for long periods of time, they are to empty their mind. This is impossible to do, as thoughts will come. Since they are not meditating on the Word, the enemy can enter their mind. They no longer have a mind of their own and before long they become emotionally and spiritually dependent on the group. It is as if they become brainwashed and cannot think for themselves. There is no incentive to leave the security of the group or even question what is going on. They accept whatever is dealt out to them.

Sometimes youth are looking for a simple structured life. They are usually distraught emotionally and are seeking help and answers to their problems. Those who do not like the rules of Christianity may be attracted to Islamism for an example, because the rules are simple and easy to follow. All they have to do is submit to the Islam's regulations, believe in God "Allah," and in Mohammed.

People who are intellectual will gravitate to cults that raise ones consciousness or enlightenment. This is particularly true of the Human Potential Movement. They look for new experiences beyond what they have already experienced. Some desire psychic power, others want divine revelation through spiritual experiences as a way to know God or to become gods themselves. This desire is the driving force of the New Agers and Mormons.

Uneducated or economically disadvantaged people are drawn to cults. We see this in a group such as the Ku Klux Klan. Those who are uneducated cannot understand the problems of society. They think America's problems are linked to unemployment, crime, and minorities. White ethnic pride motivates the Ku Klux Klan, and their solution to societies problem become prejudice and violence.

Those looking for a healing are also drawn to cults. They try to blend Christianity with the Eastern religious philosophy. An example could be Astara or the Christian Scientist. The use of familiar spirits and spirit guides are considered higher than the deity of Christ. Those searching ignore man's unregenerate nature and man's need for repentance.

They believe that God is good, so therefore good is God. In this case since evil cannot exist, any evil matter does not exist. Reality of matter must be in their minds!

Hubert F. Beck, in his book *The Cults,* gives us a few more reasons people enter cults. People have much more leisure time now, and are bored with life. Everyone is looking for happiness and fulfillment. People need to feel important and want to be committed to a cause. The church has failed in teaching commitment to Christ. Christians are to be committed to plant, sow and harvest souls. Christ calls us to this commitment. Because the church has failed, the cults move in to fill the void. Mr. Beck calls it the "unpaid bills of the church" (p.20).

Even though we are a nation under God, our churches have not taught adequate biblical knowledge. When someone entices another to enter a cult, there is little awareness that it is a cult. Frequently cults will use scriptures out of context and a person not knowledgeable of the scriptures will be easy prey. The failure of the church to teach the truth has left people vulnerable.

PART 3

Names And Philosophies
Of Various Cults

Chapter VIII

Witchcraft, Cults, New Age

The New Age Movement (New Agers) has a variety of definitions. Some would describe the movement as a network of networks. It is a loosely structured network of individuals and organizations in the political, economic, social, medical and religious areas. There is no single leader or a specific headquarter base. Their ideology is for the same goal of the one world government, and one global ecumenical religion. Generally they believe that the world problems can best be served under the United Nations and the World Constitution.

From the spiritual aspect, New Agers believe that men can become gods through spiritual evolution by cycles of reincarnation. Through their theory of enlightenment, one can become a god themselves. According to Shirley MacLaine, they believe that "god lives in each of us, that there is no right or wrong, and that through spirit guides we have the power of positive thinking."[2] Because of this concept, they can master their own destiny.

There are several areas that New Agers differ from Christianity. Since they believe that all is god, and god is all, then we will be one with dogs, stars, vegetables, cars, and any other inanimate object. Since all is god, there is no one Supreme Being. There is no accountability, for there is no god to answer to, so if one does not have to account for their actions, then sin is negated. Once sin is negated, New Age people believe they can do what ever they feel like doing with out any accountability.

New Agers believe that Jesus Christ was merely another man or prophet equal to Buddha and other religious leaders. Since they deny Jesus who is an eternal God, there is no one to be accountable to. Neither do New Agers believe in absolutes, for example, God, death, and the law of gravity are all absolutes. Any kind of moral absolutes is considered by the New Age people to be a form of spiritual stagnation.

New Age believers deny there is a heaven, hell, or judgment as literal as described in the Bible. They reason that God never made a heaven for man or a hell because man is his own creator. They can make their own heaven or hell here on earth and because of their free will, they can create either if they choose. They believe heaven is a place of final healing. In the end all is the ability to choose. They claim this choice of a final resting place can be done rationally. This is the great deception of Satan, the antichrist. It is said well in 1 John 2:18, "Little children, it is the last hour; and as you have heard that the antichrist is coming, even now many Antichrists have come, by which we know that it is the last hour." The antichrist spirit is becoming more prevalent as New Age philosophy has infiltrated society.

They also believe that man is basically good. People and especially children are known to be basically selfish. Children have to be taught to share and show respect to their parents and others. Their conscience has to be formed.

Choices are then made to choose good or evil. So many children and young people choose to do evil acts because they have not been taught the difference between right and wrong. If people are basically good, then all should choose to do good, however, we know from experience that is not generally the case.

During nurses training I had several months of training in a psychiatric unit. We had many teenagers on the ward. It was a private hospital, and the patients generally came from well-to-do families. These young men and women were so mixed up mentally and emotionally. Not knowing right from wrong, they tried everything they could afford, including drugs, sex, and alcohol. Some attempted suicide, and others committed acts of violence. How can we say people are basically good? Man is obviously prone to evil. The sinful nature of man needs help and this help comes from recognizing that we are all sinners; who are in need of a Savior. The only Savior who came to redeem sinful man is Jesus. God tells us in John 3:16, "For God so loved the world that He gave His only begotten Son, that whoever believes in Him should not perish but have everlasting life."

SPIRITISM OR SPIRITUALISM

Webster defines spiritualism as:

> 1: the view that spirit is a prime element of reality 2 a: a belief that departed spirits hold intercourse with the living usually through a medium (as by rapping or trances) b. *cap*: a movement comprising religious organizations emphasizing spiritualism (p. 843).

Spiritism was introduced in England and German around the 1850's and came to the United States between the years of 1880 to 1920. It is one of the oldest religions and it dates back to the book of Leviticus 20:6, "And the person who turns to mediums and familiar spirits, to prostitute himself with them, I will set My face against that person and cut him off from his people." To show the severity of spiritualism, God continues on in verse 27, "A man or a woman who is a medium, or who has familiar spirits, shall surely be put to death; they shall stone them with stones. Their blood shall be upon them."

The key element of Spiritualism is receiving information from a deceased person. This communication can take place by tapping or séances in a dark room. The room is dark so the ectoplasm, which is a white, foul smelling substance that comes out of the medium's mouth, is considered to be an energy form that will not function in bright light. The ectoplasm is considered essential for the spirits emanation (emit). This is typical of Satan's work of darkness as Satan hates the light because Jesus is the light of the world as stated in John 8:12, "Then Jesus spoke to them again, saying, 'I am the light of the world. He who follows Me shall not walk in darkness, but have the light of life.' "

Many of their beliefs are from spirit guides or information they receive from séances. Now days they call séances channeling and the one doing it is called a trance chandler. The information received through channeling is frequently blasphemous or profane. Spiritism does not believe in hell, no judgment, everyone is a divine child of God, and they are seeking hidden information. Deuteronomy 29:29 condemns secret things, "The secret things belong to the LORD our God, but those things which are revealed belong to us and to our children forever, that we may do all the words of this law." We are not to engage in secret things.

At a flea market I came across a lady in a booth who practiced spiritism. She was very friendly and told me up front she went to a Spiritualist church and they only did good things. She even believed she was a Christian. I shared scriptures with her that pointed out the error of spiritism. She was going to take the information to her leaders and find out if I was right. Then she told me she just stood out in the aisle of the flea market and released healing on all the people. If Satan's people can send out demonic spirits, where are the Christians going up and down the aisles at flea markets and other places praying and releasing the anointing of the Holy Spirit? Today we can call that "prayer walking" which is to stand in the gap between man and God interceding for the salvation of souls, praying for the needs of people and canceling the assignment of the evil one over the people.

MAGIC

Webster's Dictionary, describes magic as 1. a: the use of means (as charms, spells) believed to have supernatural power over natural forces, b: magic rites or incantations, 2. an extraordinary power or influences seemingly from a supernatural, 3. the art of producing illusions by legerdemain (sleight which is skill and dexterity in juggling or conjuring tricks of the hand) (p.508). Black magic seeks to harm people, usually through casting spells, using charms or potions and spiritual demonic power to achieve their selfish ends. Satanist that practice black magic can inflict disease, put people in life threatening situations, and can lead others into fateful destinies.

The Black Magic of Africa involves sorcerers, witches, ghosts, vampires, and mediums. This magic is part of their culture. They go to witch doctors, do certain incantations and may give out specific herbs, minerals or other healing potions. The witch or witch doctors would hold a pendulum in front of the potions and when the pendulum would swing toward one; they would give that potion to the person who came for help. This knowledge is not given by God but by a demonic influence. God says in Habakkuk 2:19, "Woe to him who says to wood, 'Awake!' To silent stone, 'Arise! It shall teach!' Behold, it is overlaid with gold and silver, Yet in it there is no breath at all." We are not to be led by things, only by the Holy Spirit.

People who practice black magic may also carry around fetish (an object believed among a primitive people to have magical power to protect or air its owner; *broadly*: any material object regarded with superstition or extravagant trust or reverence) (Webster p.309). They also poke pins into a voodoo doll to cause the other person pain or to get even with someone who upset them. They can cast spells, or place hexes on anyone they wish.

It has been my experience that people who become ill and the doctors cannot diagnose any disease have usually had a curse put on them. This may not always be the case; perhaps the doctor may have missed the diagnosis. When many doctors find nothing wrong, one can be reasonably sure it is a curse. In Proverbs 26:2 it says, "Like a flitting sparrow, like a flying swallow, so a curse without cause shall not alight." The only way a curse can alight is when one opens the door by sin. A Christian must walk and live with their full armor of God in place (Ephesians 6:12). They are to walk by the Spirit and try not to sin.

Witches practice white magic. I have heard them say they only do good to others in their practice. Webster defines witches as, a woman practicing the black arts: sorceress, one to possess supernatural powers especially by compact with the devil or a familiar (p.1025). By this definition, witches do more that practice white magic. Familiar according to Webster, "Is a spirit often embodied in an animal and held to attend and serve or guard a person" (p.301). So from these definitions, white magic has a hard time staying white, it is soon to become gray. Usually those who practice white magic do it for their own gain. They are usually people who desire fame or power and stop at nothing to get it. This is why there is never a gray area for very long. Once the enemy has influence in their lives, he will try to take them into lower depths of depravity. Before long it can become black magic, which can turn into satanic worship. John 10:10 says, "The thief does not come except to steal, and to kill, and to destroy. I have come that they may have life, and that they may have it more abundantly."

There is also sympathetic magic. It is based on the principle that "like produces like." In other words, some things that have a resemblance to each other in shape have a magical resemblance to each other, or a have a magical relationship. If two similar things (person, place, or object) occur, there is a magical connection.

Another form of magic is Liturgy of magic. Many times this form of magic is parallel to Christian liturgy. In a magic ceremony, four elements are used namely, charm, invocation, symbolic action, and a fetish. With the invocation the black magic is invoking Satan instead of God. Usually the person has signed himself over to the devil with his blood. The charm puts magical powers into operation. It mimics the Bible, prayer and the symbolic action might be forms of prayer or laying on of hands. A fetish (amulet or talisman) is a magical charmed object that carries magical powers. It could be a good luck charm, a rabbit's foot or such thing as a medal.

The last type of magic is lycanthropic. They believe that under certain conditions, people can turn into animals. A man can do this temporarily or permanently. This is where the idea of werewolf comes from. The concept is perhaps legendary or superstitious.

All of magic speaks of darkness. We are clearly warned not to walk in darkness. In 1 John 1:5 it states, "This is the message which we have heard from Him and declare to you, that God is light and in Him is no darkness at all." I like what

John says in Chapter 3:18-21, "He who believes in Him is not condemned; but he who does not believe is condemned already, because he has not believed in the name of the only begotten Son of God. And this is the condemnation that the light has come into the world, and men loved darkness rather than light, because their deeds were evil. For everyone practicing evil hates the light and does not come to the light, lest his deeds should be exposed. But he who does the truth comes to the light, that his deeds may be clearly seen, that they have been done in God." There can be no doubt that we are to live in the light as God makes it very clear in His inspired Word.

HALLOWEEN

Back in the seventh century Christians commemorated the early Christians who died by celebrating "Hallows Eve." This was the night before what Roman Catholics called "All Saints Day." By the 10th century more witchcraft was practiced than Christianity and the feast became a secular custom.

The ancient druids were from the Celtic priesthood appearing in Irish and Welsh sagas as well as in Christian legends were magicians and wizards (*Webster* p.255). They honored their god Samhaim (pagan lord of the dead). Druids believed that October 31 (Halloween) was the eve of the day of death that was celebrated on November 1st. They believed that the spirits of the dead return to their former homes to visit their relatives. If the living relatives did not provide food for them, they would bring them and their community bad luck. Jack was believed to be one of these spirits wondering between heaven and earth trying to get to heaven. Because of this belief they carved out turnips and put a candle in it to outwit the devil and to keep Jack from going to hell. The jack-o-lantern is the symbol of a damned soul. The lighted pumpkin today is to frighten evil spirits such as witches, goblins, ghosts, and other spiritual forces away.

Christians can be very comfortable with the festive pumpkin. We can take back what the enemy has perverted. Look at the rich, colorful pumpkin as a symbol of a Christian. When God clean us up, He is pulling out all the unnecessary seeds of darkness hidden inside of us. The final cleansing comes when He puts the light of Jesus inside of us, which causes us to smile. The smile is carved in our life forever for we know we will be with Jesus.

The Halloween witch's name comes from the Saxon word "Wicca" which means "wise one." Witches wear black because they are believed to celebrate the festival of the dead. When witches were to fly off to celebrate one of their eight yearly Sabbaths, they needed to cross over brooks. The symbol of women in the middle ages was a broom. They believed that angels and devils could fly and also witches. From this the image of a witch on a broom was born.

With the idea of witches and brooms, came the "trick or treat" tradition. It was a pagan custom to put food and drink outside the door for the wondering spirits in order to appease them. It was believed if the spirits were satisfied, they would leave the home and then the home would be at peace. Some mischievous children would go around and steal the food set out for the spirits. The concept of, "You either give me a treat, or I'll play a trick on you" became a custom. When children dressed up in costumes they believed they could scare evil spirits away. Some costumes and decorations have to do with skulls, skeletons and corpses which are part of the celebration of death.

We chose to celebrate the life of Jesus. Jesus came that we may have life more abundantly. He says in John 10:10, "The thief does not come to steal, and to kill, and to destroy. I have come that they may have life, and that they may have it more abundantly." It is our privilege to make the right choice.

The pagan Celts believed that bats and owls could

communicate with the dead. The bat is a significant symbol because of its unique ability to find its prey in the dark. This is why the bat has had a frightening reputation as having occult power. The vampire bat also drinks blood. The owl is a creature of the night. Most cultic or satanic rituals take place at night. The eyes of owls are glassy and large making them appear mysterious and possibly attract other spirits. One can choose to walk in the light rather than darkness. It is simply stated in 1 John 1:6,7 "If we say that we have fellowship with Him, and walk in darkness, we lie and do not practice truth. But if we walk in the light as He is in the light, we have fellowship with one another, and the blood of Jesus Christ His Son cleanses us from all sin."

The cat of Halloween was believed to be a symbol of evil (familiar) spirits that are in animals. The black cat was said to become a horse to take people to worship on Halloween. Others believed that black cats had been humans at one time and now changed into animals because of the evil they once did. The magic of cat eyes led some to believe that cats had strong medium powers. A Christian need not have any fear of God's created animals. We can love our animals including black cats as a gift from God.

Some witches were asked if they celebrated Samhaim (Halloween) to this very day.. Their response was published in the *Cult Watch Response,* (October 1988, Vol. 1, No. 1) as follows:

"Yes, many followers of various pagan religions, such as Druids, and Wiccans (witches), observe this day as a religious festival. They view it as a memorial day for their dead friends similar to the national holiday of Memorial Day in May. It is still a night to practice various forms of divination concerning future events. Also, it is a time to ...initiate new projects."

Weeks prior to Halloween, Witches, Satanists, have been known to kidnap children, dogs, cats and other animals for their satanic worship. During their ceremony on this unholy night, they will drink, dance, cast spells and curses, conjure up dead spirits, engage in sexual orgies, induct new members as well as offering human and animal sacrifices. They cover their tracks by cremating the remains or burying them in deeply dug graves. They usually hide out in a secluded building, wooded area, or in a cemetery.

Many children are drawn to the occult because they have been exposed to the elements of cultic practices through participation in Halloween. Children desire to do what everyone else is doing. Parents will want to do what Proverbs 22:6 says, "Train up a child in the way he should go, and when he is old he will not depart from it." Even when parents substitute a Bible party on that day they are still honoring the witches Sabbath by celebrating on their holiday.

One time I had a Christian couple call me for help. Their little five year-old adopted boy kept saying he was going to serve Satan. They had prayed for him and with him. He even gave his heart to the Lord. I asked them if they ever anointed him with oil and consecrated him to the Lord like it says in Exodus 40:9 "And you shall take the anointing oil, and anoint the tabernacle and all that is in it; and you shall hallow it and all its utensils, and it shall be holy." The parents did this after he went to sleep. The next morning he got up and said he was going to serve Jesus. On his own he destroyed all the Halloween pictures he had cut out. The spiritual tie had been broken. Satan is real but we do not need to fear him. He was defeated on the cross of Jesus Christ. Satan has to bow at the name of Jesus. We know from Philippians 2:10-11, "That at the name of Jesus every knee should bow, of those in heaven, and of those on earth, and of those under the earth, and that every tongue should confess that Jesus is Lord, to the glory of God the Father."

When Witches or Satanists sacrifice a child or animal, they are imitating the shed blood of Christ for us, as He was our Supreme sacrifice. He is the only one we can come to for saving our lives (John 3:16). There are no tricks to Halloween. God's treat for us is His eternal plan for our lives. We are all sinners and separated from God. It is verified in Roman 3:23, "For all have sinned and fall short of the glory of God." He is the only one to whom we can come to receive eternal life.

For anyone to have assurance about getting to heaven, all we have to do is admit that we have sinned. For we all have sinned (Romans 3:23). We can invite Jesus to come into our heart and be Lord of our life. Immediately share our decision with another Christian or even with anyone else not yet saved. Tell them what Jesus has done for us. Begin attending a church that teaches the Word of God. Ask to be water baptized. Begin reading the Bible each day and let God speak to us through what He says in His Word. Pray daily for others as well as for one self.

We are admonished to refrain from the darkness of this world. This is clearly confirmed in 2 Corinthians 6:14-17, which says, "Do not be unequally yoked together with unbelievers. For what fellowship has righteousness with lawlessness? And what communion has light with darkness? And what accord has Christ with Belial? Or what part has a believer with an unbeliever? And what agreement has the temple of God with idols? For you are the temple of the living God. As God has said: 'I will dwell in them and walk among them. I will be their God, and they shall be My people.' " We are to remain separate from anything to do with Satan and his works. The evils of witchcraft are denounced repeatedly in God's Word in Deuteronomy 12:31,18:10-14, 1 Chronicles 10:13, 2 Chronicles 33:6, 1 Samuel 15:23, Exodus 22:18, Leviticus 19:26,31, 20:27, Isaiah 8:19,19:8,12,13, 47:9, 2 Kings 7:17, 21:6:23,24, Jeremiah 27:9,10, Malachi

3:5, Acts 13:6-10, Galatians 5:19,20, and Revelations 1:8. We are to serve none other than the Most High God if we expect to get to heaven. The first couple of commandments in Exodus 20 2,3, tells us, "I am the Lord your God, who brought you out of Egypt, out of the house of bondage. You shall have no other gods before me."

GOTHIC MOVEMENT

Today we have a new culture that revolves around violence and death. The majority of our younger people are taught there are no absolutes. Their philosophy is "if it feels good do it," leading to hopelessness and despair. Some youth walk around without purpose. This subculture has led some to the Gothic Movement.

One can easily pick out a teen involved in the Gothic Movement. They usually dress in a black long coat, wear white makeup, may have a strange hairstyle or hair dyed an unusual color, sometimes have fangs, and they are preoccupied with death. They want to do something different and latch on to the bizarre. Besides their dress they listen to specific types of music, art, and literature.

Some of their music comes from groups such as the Banshees, Siouxsie, The Damned, Marilyn Manson and others involved in Satanism or Gothic culture. The Gothic's read books on spells, tarot cards and literature about Satanism, vampires and even blood sharing in one form or another. Blood sharing is one of the practices carried out during satanic rituals.

Kim Ferrell of the Christian Broadcasting Network interviewed Hank Hangraaff who hosts a radio show called, "The Bible Answer Man." He says the kids are preoccupied with the dark side of life. They are usually intelligent and introspective, but there is no real meaning in their lives. When there is no standard of right or wrong, there is no standard.

Everything is subjective; there is no meaning to life, so that being the case, it does not matter how they dress or act; all is meaningless. Mr. Ferrell says, "That's part of the nihilism of our culture, and that's why we have to show people that there are objective verities, and that if you live a life of believing there aren't, then you have total chaos and confusion"[3] Many of our youth today are confused.

The movement is considered to be a harmless form of self-expression. Many Goths lives were wounded and now are trying to find meaning in this life. They are obsessed with the darkness of Satan, despair and death. The two young men that shot thirteen people and themselves at Columbine High School in 1999 sometimes dressed like the Goths did. The group they belonged to was called the Trench Coat Mafia. Obviously, the Gothic Movement is not such an innocent and harmless subculture.

Christine O'Donnell who is the president of the Savior's Alliance for Lifting the Truth (SALT) is one of the groups that ministers to these youth. She comments that Satan is behind this culture. We know he comes to cheat, steal, and destroy as many people as he can (John 10:10). She says, "These young people are broken and wounded. They need something to latch on to. They identify with the brokenness and the darkness in our own souls apart from God. The Gothic Movement validates that." She commented that the Gothic scene was born out of the punk rock movement of the 1970's. Her opinion is that the movement is focused on the dead. Young people are attracted to it because it gives them a sense of belonging.

All souls are in darkness until they come to the light. God is an absolute, He is truth. He rewards the good, and punishes the wicked. There is no hope outside of Jesus. He is ones hope of glory. Colossians 1:27 is encouraging when it says, "To them God willed to make known what are the riches of the glory of this mystery among the

Gentiles: which is Christ in you, the hope of glory." He is the only way!

Parents and Christians need to spend time to help those who are lost and looking for self-identity. Self-fulfillment and identity comes from the One who wants to reside within. We are whole and complete in Jesus. 1 Timothy 4:10 says it well, "For to this end we both labor and suffer reproach, because we trust in the living God, who is the Savior of all men, especially of those who believe." Everyone wants to believe in something. Why not believe in the truth? "Jesus said, to him 'I am the way, the truth, and the life. No one comes to the Father except through Me' " (John 14:6).

UFO'S

UFO's (unidentified flying objects) get their name of flying saucers from Ken Arnold. In 1947 he was flying his private plane around Mount Rainier, Washington, at an altitude of 9,2000 feet. The afternoon was sunny when he saw blue and white flashes in front of him. There was a group of UFO's that appeared as dazzling objects gliding over the mountaintops in formation. He said they flew like saucers and from that remark the newspaper reporters coined the name of UFO's as flying saucers.

Back in the 1950's and 1960's records of UFO the government kept sightings. The recorded sightings were called "Project Blue Book." It was an unclassified operation but kept very secret. The government does not know what UFO's are. They cannot be shot down, duplicated, communicated with or know the purposes and places they will appear. Regardless of their purpose, they cannot be ignored. The military calls UFO's a conventional phenomenon. The Air Force tries to debunk all sightings reported; neither do they have any significant explanation for the appearances of UFO's.

Some of those who have been abducted by aliens were told their purpose of extraterrestrials was to help humans' ascent to become gods. Our purpose is not to become god but to worship and declare His glory as stated in Revelations 7:9,10. We are to believe God's Word and have nothing to do with spiritism. Anything to do with the spirit world that is not inspired by the Holy Spirit, is from the demonic spirit world. God has warned us in Leviticus 19:31 when He said, "Give no regard to mediums and familiar spirits; do not seek after them, to be defiled by them: I am the LORD your God." There is much psychic phenomenon going on with those who say they have seen or experienced being transported in UFO's. Spiritism seeks to obtain knowledge from sources other than from God and this is akin to spiritism.

Dr. J. Allen Hynek was an authority on UFO's. Before he died he gave two assumptions. One was that another civilization from where the UFO's originate must be more advanced than ours and we would then be inferior in intelligence. Secondly, he admitted that the mind-matter could be a connection. Being a scientist, he had no proof of either concept so he concluded the theory that UFO's are from another dimension or a parallel reality.[4]

Aliens are believed to be humanoids, nonhumanoids, and hybrids, which are a cross between aliens and humans. It is believed aliens have attacked animals by sucking out their blood, take out their rectum in a clean-cut circular fashion or remove their sex organs. These attacks are similar to the practices that Satanists do during their cultic satanic rituals.[5] People who have been in contact with aliens are reported to be instilled with fear, anxiety, and feel controlled by them. This is another reason that UFO's are considered to come from Satan's underworld because God has not given us a spirit of fear (2 Timothy 1:7). There are three hundred and sixty five "fear-nots" in the Bible, one for every day of the year. In God there should be no fear.

In Bob Larson's book, *UFO's and the Alien Agenda* has four possible conclusions to explain UFO's. The first one is that there is evidence to show something definitely is happening as some UFO's are real. There existence can have an empirical scientific explanation. The second conclusion is that some cases of UFO's cannot be explained. They appear to be a spiritual or nonmaterial in nature. Thirdly, if the UFO's were man made for financial gain, the truth would have leaked out by now. Lastly, in a special act of divine grace, God created heaven and earth. It is believed then that the aliens cannot be from another planet or solar system.[6]

Satan could easily appear in the form of aliens. God sent an angel to announce the birth of Jesus to Mary. Since demons are fallen angels, they can also appear in other forms such as men. Elisha went up in a chariot of fire as stated in 2 Kings 2:11, so Satan could counterfeit UFO's.

We know from Matthew Chapter 24 that whoever believes in Jesus will be removed at a blink of an eye. Verse 40 confirms it, "Then two men will be in a field; one will be taken and the other left." The Word in verse 42 tells us to "Watch therefore, for you do not know what hour your Lord is coming." I believe it is possible that Satan is trying to imitate what God will do in the last days. The New Agers stole the rainbow for their symbol. God has given it to His people as a sign of His promise never to flood the earth again (Genesis 9:13). Satan counterfeits, perverts and steals from His creator.

People can have paranormal experiences such as out of body experiences or astral projection as described by Dr. Rebecca Brown in her book, *He Came To Set The Captives Free* (p.15). All these experiences are forms of spiritism. God condemns this type of behavior. We see this when King Saul went to the Witch of Endor and she conjured up Samuel the prophet's spirit (1 Samuel Chapter 28). It appears that UFO's could be considered to be a similar spiritual phenomenon and must be avoided.

ASTROLOGY

Astrology is defined, by Webster as "The divination of the supposed influences of the stars upon human affairs and terrestrial events by their positions and aspects. Sometimes astrology is also called astronomy. Astronomy is the science of the celestial bodies and of their magnitudes, motions, and constitution or a treatise on this science" (p. 54-55).

According to a George Gallop poll, one in five adults in America believe in astrology (32 million). Eight out of ten people know what their sign is. Many cable TV, newspapers and magazines carry horoscopes. Even former President Regan's wife Nancy believed in astrology. In Isaiah 47: 13-15 it says, "You are wearied in the multitude of your counsels; let now the astrologers, the stargazers, and the monthly prognosticators stand up and save you from what shall come upon you. Behold, they shall be as stubble, the fire shall burn them; they shall not deliver themselves from the power of the flame; it shall not be a coal to be warmed by, nor a fire to set before! Thus shall they be to you with whom you have labored, Your merchants from your youth; they shall wander each one to his quarter. No one shall save you." From this scripture we understand that we are not to live according to horoscopes. One should not even read them because they influence one subconsciously.

Astrology goes as far back as the ancient Babylonian Empire. Babylonians believed there was the influence of the sun upon the earth as well as the moon having an influence on the seas. This led to worshipping the planets as gods rather than the God who made them. In Bob Larson's *New Book of Cults,* it is believed that one of the reason for the building of the Tower of Babel was to survey the stars. They were trying to determine their destiny through the stars rather than through God (p.142). Since the Babylonians were seeking knowledge apart from God, God's judgment came on them. God confused their language and stopped the tower building. Genesis 11:7-8 declares "Come, let Us go down and there confuse their language, that they may not understand one another's speech. So the Lord scattered them abroad from there over the face of all the earth, and they ceased building the city." What ever their motive was, God did not approve.

Another explanation comes from Warren Wiersbe's book, *Be Basic*:

> The tower they built at Babel was what is known as a "ziggurat." ...these large structures which were built primarily for religious purposes. ...at the top was a shrine dedicated to a god or goddess. In building the structure the people were not trying to climb to heaven to dethrone God; rather they hoped that the god or goddess they worshiped would come down from heaven to meet them. The structure and the city were called "Babel" which means "the gate of the gods." (p.125)

The scientists also know the inaccuracy of astrology. They issued a statement quoted by Bob Larson in his book, *Larson's New Book of Cults*. It says, "The time has come to challenge directly and forcefully the pretentious claims of astrological charlatans. It is simply a mistake to imagine that the forces exerted by stars and planets at the moment of birth can in any way shape our future" (p. 140). In spite of this, astrology continues to expand.

Horoscopes began at the time when scientists thought the earth was flat and it was the center of the universe. We now know that the sun is the center of the universe and discredits their theory. There is on opinion by some scientists that the earth spun off its axis, and Zodiac has shifted so the present horoscope readings are off by about a month. According to these scientists this is just one example. It is believed there are many other errors in astrology signs as well.

God says in Deuteronomy 18:9-13, "When you come into the land which the LORD your God is giving you, you shall not learn to follow the abominations of those nations. There shall not be found among you anyone who makes his son or his daughter pass through the fire, or one who practices witchcraft, or a soothsayer, or one who interprets omens, or a sorcerer, or one who conjures spells, or a medium, or a spiritist, or one who calls up the dead. For all who do these things are an abomination to the LORD, and because of these abominations the LORD your God drives them out from before you. You shall be blameless before the LORD your God." We are to worship God and not His creation. Psalm 19:1 states, "The heavens declare the glory of God; and the firmament shows His handiwork." Knowledge is to be sought from the Creator and not His creation. Astrology tries to take us away from our faith in God in whom we should trust.

Chapter IX

Eastern Religions

HINDUISM

Hinduism is one of the oldest false religions in the world. It is a very complex religious system that has changed over the years. There seems to be a family of religions dating back as far as 1400 B.C.

Hinduism is a religion that seeks the truth. This is the thread of all religions, but how they believe and apply the truth varies. In their Vedas (collection of wisdom books), the "truth is one, they call him by different names." The Vedas also includes hymns of praise to gods, a guide for practicing ritual rights (magical spells and incantations), as well as teachings on religious truth and doctrine.

There are various Hindu Scriptures. They are divided into two classes. The first one is the *sruti,* which means, "what is heard," or the canonical revealed scriptures. These refer to the eternal truths of religion, which the *rishis* (seers) saw and heard. The other is the *smriti,* which are the traditional semi canonical writings. This is "what is remembered."

A unique feature of the Hindu religion is the caste system. They believe that Brahma (Supreme Deity) created Manu, the first man. From his head came the most holy people. From Manu's hands came the Kshatriyas, these are warriors or rulers and upper middle class. Out of Manu's thighs came Vaisyas, these are merchants and farmers. All the remaining people came out of his feet called the Sudras. Sudras are the lower class and were to serve the upper class. They could not be included in the religious rituals or be permitted to study the Vedas. Due to this belief in Manu, the Hindus accept the fact that the caste system was divinely inspired.

Hindus believe works through religious duty can save them. The way of knowledge that infers human suffering is based on ignorance and only the intellectual few make it through specific steps. They must not see themselves as a separate and real entity, but part of the whole Brahman (eternal trimutri called Brahma, Shina, and Krishna). This reflects a devotion to a deity by acts of worship. It is also carried out in their love of their family and obedience to their master. An explanation of their way of devotion can be found in the Hindu scripture called *Bhagavad Gita* (The Song of the Lord). It is a philosophical conversation between the Lord God Krishna and the warrior Arjuna.

In Christianity we have a personal God, Jesus. In Romans 5:6 it states, "For when we were still without strength, in due time Christ died for the ungodly." He is a personal God laying down His life in love for us. We are all ungodly without a Savior.

In Hinduism they also believe in their doctrines of karma and reincarnation. Reincarnation cannot cleanse us from the guilt of sin. Jesus Christ is our only Savior. Hebrews 1:3 tells it very clearly when it states, "Who being the brightness of His glory and the express image of His person, and upholding all things by the word of His power, when He had by Himself purged our sins, sat down at the right hand of the Majesty on high." Jesus is the hope of glory, He is our future and one day we will rest with Him.

Reincarnation is the opposite of a Christian's belief in the resurrection of Christ and our personal resurrection some day. History proves that Jesus rose from the dead in Jerusalem on the third after His death. No other religious leader has risen from the dead. This is the reason to prove that He is God! We know we will be resurrected from Acts 24:15 which says, "I have hope in God, which they themselves also accept, that there will be a resurrection of the dead, both of the just and the unjust."

Reincarnation does not negate judgment at the time of death. It tells us in Hebrews 9:27 that, "And as it is appointed for men to die once, but after this the judgment." This also proves that during our lifetime, we are accountable to God. We must seek to follow God's principles, commandments, and precepts, if we want to have eternal happiness, and peace with the Lord. Man will not have a second chance after death or to come back again. The Hindu religion does not acknowledge their need for a Savior.

Today New Age people have assumed the philosophy of the Hindu religion. It has greatly infiltrated into the medical field. An example is Ayurveda, which dates back over 4000 years. One facet of Ayurveda healing is to meditate. The form of meditation most frequently used is transcendental meditation (TM). The founder of (TM) Mararishi Mahesh Yogi, a Hindu monk, claims his form of meditation is not a religion. Maharishe means "great seer" and Yogi means "Master of Yoga." He had a divine "teacher" by the name of Guru Dev, from which he learned to teach transcendental meditation. His followers in Austin, Texas had this to say as reported in the *Dallas Morning News,* February 4, 1990:

"A New Age style community southwest of Austin that will be known as the City of Immortals." These visionaries have conceived of a world wide movement fashioned of "harmonious, largely self-contained residential areas that are free of pollution, crime and anxiety." Developers state they intend to establish a community health facility designed to "balance the whole person—mind, body, behavior and environment. The goal is to prevent disease and promote perfect health and longevity creating a disease-free society."

In the medical field one needs to be careful to know of the belief of the health care practitioner. By understanding, we can try to give the truth of God's Word to them. Basically everyone is hungry for God and is trying to fill the void with what they think is right. Jesus is the Way, the Truth and the Life. No one comes to the Father in heaven except through Jesus (John 14:6).

YOGA

The term Yoga comes from the Sanikrit word *yuj*, which means, "to join." It is union with a god. The god of Yoga is an impersonal god who is on the earth in the form of energy. An impersonal deity such as energy cannot achieve spiritual union with the true God; it is achieved through a personal relationship with Jesus and the Holy Spirit.

People are drawn into the Yoga cult through the offer of exercise. Many people are stressed out, overweight, and concerned about their physical appearance. Yoga offers a less strenuous method of restoring life from a sedentary form of life style, to a more ascetic youthfulness. What they do not realize is that it is a Hindu religion going back as far as 5000 years. Every posture in Yoga was designed to worship the

Hindu god Krishna.

The aim of Yoga is to achieve *Brahma*. Webster defines *Brahma* as the ultimate ground of all being in Hinduism or the creator god of the Hindu sacred triad (p.101). In other words the exercises and meditations of Yoga are designed to align ones body to absorb the cosmic force. By heightening god consciousness, one elevates the awareness of the spiritual body. They assume that man is intrinsically good. We know from the fall of Adam and Eve that we are not intrinsically good and that man needs to be redeemed from the fall. It is very clear in John 3:1-21, Jesus tells us that we need a savior. He gave His life, and if one believes in Him, we will be saved.

We cannot communicate with God through various postures and an altered state of consciousness. Different positions cannot bring body parts to a specific level of spirituality or altered awareness. We are to bow our knees to God alone. It is very clear in Romans 11:4, "But what does the divine response say to him? I have reserved Myself seven thousand men who have not bowed the knee to Baal." We communicate with God when we humble ourselves on our knees and pray.

It is only the shed blood of Christ that we can come into union with Him and be able to carry out God's will in our life. Through this surrender one will relieve stress, find peace, and the bodily functions are more apt to be restored than through Yoga exercises. Jesus said, "Peace I leave with you, My peace I give to you; not as the world gives do I give to you. Let not your heart be troubled, neither let it be afraid." (John 14:27a). Jesus goes on to say in John 14:30, "I will no longer talk much with you, for the ruler of this world is coming, and he has nothing in Me." This says it all. No matter what people try in the natural or through the demonic supernatural, there will be no true peace except that which Our Lord and Savior can give.

THEOSOPHY

The term Theosophy comes from the Greek word *theosophia,* means divine wisdom. "Its philosophy is a contemporary presentation of a perennial wisdom underlying the world's religions, science, and philosophies."[7] Webster says Theosophy is a belief about God and the world held to be based on mystical insight. This is a belief of a modern movement originating in the United States in 1875 and following the Buddhist and Brahmanism theories of pantheistic evolution and reincarnation (p.916). In other words, God is a form of emanation. Webster describes emanation as the world in a series of hierarchically descending radiations from the godhead through intermediate stages to matter (p.269). According to their belief, the Divine is to be emanated in this manner.

The stages of Theosophy are called by different names. Some are enlightenment, (negation of one's rational faculties), transcendental bliss, heightened awareness, nirvana, god realization, satori, expanded consciousness, or cosmic consciousness. Those that believe in emanation besides the Theosophy religion are the Hindus, Buddhists, Unity, and Scientology. God is reduced to an impersonal deity by all of them.

The founder of Theosophy was a woman, Madame Helena Petrovna Blavatsky. She was born in 1831 in Russia, of aristocratic German descent. As a teenager she was wild and without any moral control. She had psychic tendencies as a very young girl. After two marriages and many lovers, she gave birth to an illegitimate child.

Helen traveled extensively and when visiting in the United States, she became involved in Spiritualism. While in New York, Col. Henry Steel Olcott joined her in her occult practices. William Quan Judge also joined her and they formed the Theosophical Society in 1875. She wrote her first book, *Isis Unveiled*, which became the main document of Theosophy, and later she wrote, *The Secret Doctrine*. Their United States headquarters is in Wheaton, Il. They claim about 6,000 members in the United States and about 25,000 members in 60 countries.

The Theosophical Society has what they call the "Three Declared Objects." They are:

1. To form a nucleus of the Universal Brotherhood of humanity without distinction of race, creed, sex, caste, or color.
2. To encourage the comparative study of religion, philosophy, and science.
3. To investigate unexplained laws of nature and the powers latent in humanity.[8]

These objectives can be very appealing, especially to those who hold a universal view. One must delve into their teaching more at length to see the errors.

When in Tibet Helena bragged about making contact with disembodied higher spiritual beings called *Mahatmas*. She gives credit to the *Mahatmas* (spirit guides) for directing her through letters, messages, and her entire life. One is to be led only by the Holy Spirit.

When one studies Scripture and the attributes of God, Theosophy does not come anywhere near the God of the Bible. Theosophy denies the deity of Christ and that He died for the whole world (1 John 2:2). In Colossians 2:10, it states, "You are complete in Him, who is the head of all principality and power." In Acts 20:28 it disproves the concept of "karma" and reincarnation, by saying, "Therefore take heed to yourselves and to all the flock, among which the Holy Spirit has made you overseers, to shepherd the church of God which He purchased with His own blood." Christ is the only way.

Theosophy puts God the Father on the same level as

Buddha, and Vishnu, which are pagan gods. Their prayer is "concentrated thought" where as the Bible explains what we are to do in Philippians 4:6-7 where it says, "Be anxious for nothing, but in everything by prayer and supplication, with thanksgiving, let your requests be made known to God; and the peace of God, which surpasses all understanding, will guard your hearts and minds through Christ Jesus." In regard to death they believe the more they suffer here the easier their lives will be in the next reincarnated life. When a Christian dies, they are absent from the body and present with the Lord (2 Corinthians 5:8).

ANANDA MARGA YOGA SOCIETY

The founder of Ananda Marga Yoga Society is Maha-Guru (Avatar—incarnation of God, also called "teachers" or "way showers"). Maha-Guru goes by the name of Shrii Shrii Anandamutim. He is also known as Probhat Ranjam Sarkav.

The philosophy of this society is a path of joy and bliss. It follows closely to yoga principles and practices of a guru. A guru is a personal religious teacher and spiritual guide in Hinduism. They also practice mantic type meditation. Mantra means in Hinduism or Buddhism a sacred word or formula as in incantation.

According to Bob Larson in *Larson's New Book of Cults*, he explains that Ananda Marga ("joy") have a path of joy and bliss along with yogic principles and practices. They will do the Kiirtan dancing, (swaying with raised arms) and as they dance they chant "Baba Nam Kevalam" which means, "the cosmic father is everywhere." The purpose of the dance is to increase spiritual vibration to help one realize that, "all of creation is a manifestation of the Lord. They also do *kundoline* yoga and charitable service to others in order to "break down the ego-bound mind." This tactic is used to entice people to join them (p.110). They do not realize that we cannot partake of a cup of Jesus and a cup of Satan. 1 Corinthians 10:21 says, it clearly, "You cannot drink the cup of the Lord and the cup of demons; you cannot partake of the Lords table and of the table of demons."

The Yoga society has about 4000 members. Most of the members are in Australia and they pursue the way of joy.[9] What they do not know is that true joy comes from the heart of God. The word of God says in John 16:22, "Therefore you now have sorrow; but I will see you again and your heart will rejoice, and your joy no one will take from you."

We are to love the LORD our God with our whole being, Deuteronomy 6:5 says, "You shall love the LORD your God with all your heart, with all your soul, and with all your strength. And these words which I command you today shall be in your heart." This can mean dancing like David did before the Ark of the Covenant in 2 Samuel 6:14, "Then David danced before the LORD with all his might; and David was wearing a linen ephod." This can also mean raising our hands in praise of our God. 1 Timothy 2:8 declares, "I desire therefore that the men pray everywhere, lifting up holy hands, without wrath and doubting." Satan is trying to steal God's praise and worship for himself by using other religions. We are to have no part of them.

BUDDHISM

There are several different types of Buddhism and each type has a different leader. Siddharta Gautama started his belief around 500 B.C. Siddharta was a prince born in the kingdom of Shakya. He lived a life of pleasure and rarely left his estate. When he ventured outside the palace, he saw how the less fortunate lived and became disenchanted with his wealthy life style. Siddharta left his wife and began his search to seek the peace of nirvana and find the cause of suffering. He began to study with two Yoga Masters. Siddharta was dissatisfied with the Yoga Masters and turned to asceticism. He deprived himself of food, often eating only one grain of rice, or his own excrement. On his 35th birthday, he was sitting under a *Pipal Bodhi* (wisdom) tree. He refused to move until he "attained understanding." Later he claimed his divine eye was quickened and he became "Buddha," the enlightened one.

Buddha was indifferent to the origin of man and would not recognize any supreme deity; neither did he believe in a heaven or hell. He maintained heaven and hell were just conditions and not real places. He preached that man has no soul but rather exists in five conditions. They are pure ideas, consciousness, will, feeling, and body. He taught that "birth is sorrow, age is sorrow, and death is sorrow." Suffering was a result of man's desire to seek pleasure in the existence of this life.

He maintained three premises of truth. They were existence is suffering, desire causes suffering, and ridding all desire ends suffering. This led him to a fourth conclusion of truth namely; his innovative "Eightfold Path" can eradicate desire. Buddha held that there were five obstacles to hinder ones enlightenment. They are pride, sloth, malice, lust, and doubt. He also believed in three refuges, which are the refuge in Buddha, the *Sangha,* and in the Dharma. These have to be affirmed by those who joined his Brotherhood of Monks (*Sangha*). Those who joined the Brotherhood of Monks also had to observe five "have-nots." The Monks were not to own any gold or silver, not to sleep on a comfortable bed, not to apply any perfume, or personal adornment, not to be present at any dramatic or musical performance, and not to eat after midday. Besides that they were not to kill, steal, lie, drink liquor or commit adultery.

The Buddhists hold to three principles that are to guide them as they are striving for *nirvana* (final spiritual fulfillment). The first principle designates thirty-one planes of existence. The second principle believes that one's karma determines his spiritual plane. The third and last principle was to achieve complete awareness through practicing contemplation or meditation.

Padina Sambhava introduced Buddhism to Tibet in 747 A.D. He was a pagan exorcist that mixed Hindu and Buddhist belief, with spells and secretive ceremonies. During these pagan ceremonies they performed sexual acts with ritualistic consumption of wine, meat, fish, and parched grains. They also designed prayer wheels with inscribed litanies. They instituted a priesthood of "superior ones,"called *lamas*. At this time they adopted *Mantras* and *Mandala,* which are mystic diagrams. The center of the *Mandalai* was believed to be the center of the universe.

The late Dalai Lama who was a Buddhist had six million people following him. They worshipped him as a "god king." His real name was Tenzin Gyatso, which means "radiant oceans of wisdom." He ruled until 1951 when the Chinese Communists invaded Tibet.

When Dalai Lama fled the Communists and went to India in 1959, he took 110,000 refugees with him. The western countries became fascinated with his views. The major Tibetan Buddhist text, *The Tibetan Book of the Dead,* became the guide to higher thought by the drug culture in the 1960's. According to the doctrine taught in this book, the soul of a dead lama passes into a newborn boy, and this is what is believed to have happened to the present Dalai Lama.

Two Japanese Buddhists developed Zen Buddhism in another form. Zen Buddhists meditate by sitting in an erect (lotus) position, the mouth firmly closed and the eyes open staring at a pool, flower, rock or some point of concentration. The purpose is to think neither good nor evil. This type of meditation is designed to lead the mind into intuitive truth. One may be defined Zen as concentration with an empty mind. Dr. T. Suzuki, a foremost Western Zen master says, "Zen teaches nothing."

A sect such as Buddhism believing in demonic ceremonialism and the propitiation of spirits constitutes witchcraft. According to Deuteronomy 18:10-13, this practice is strictly forbidden. The verse states, "There shall not be found among you anyone who makes his son or his daughter pass through the fire, or one who practices witchcraft, or a soothsayer, or one who interprets omens, or a sorcerer, or one who conjures spells, or a medium, or a spiritist, or one who calls up the dead. For all who do these things are an abomination to the LORD, and because of these abominations the LORD your God drives them out from before you. You shall be blameless before the LORD your God." The Zen meditation is also contrary to Christ's teaching. He tells us to have the mind of Christ. In the Old Testament Book of Isaiah 26:3 it states "You will keep him in perfect peace, whose mind is stayed on You, because he trusts in You." This is a sharp contrast to the introspection of Buddhism.

Their belief also leads to social indifference of those around them. Jesus said to love our neighbor as ourselves. This is the greatest commandment. Matthew 22:37-39 states, "Jesus said to him 'You shall love the LORD your God with all your heart, with all your soul, and with all your mind. This is the first and great commandment.'" Living in a Buddhist monastery is not carrying out this principle. Neither are they serving or loving the true God.

TAOISM

Taoism (pronounced "dowism") was founded by Lao-tse in 604 B.C. He was born in China and given this name because it means "old child." It is a myth that he was born old and in fact some scholars doubt he ever existed. Others believed he dropped out of political life and wrote the Bible of Taoism called, *Tao* (way) *Te* (virtu*e*) *Ching* or simply called "The Tao" or "The Way of Virtue."

The doctrine of Taoism had "Three Jewels." They are compassion, moderation and humility. Taoism also teaches if events and things that are permitted to happen in natural harmony with the macrocosmic force, peace will follow. They are to avoid all aggression and do what is natural and spontaneous. A Chinese philosopher called Chuang Tzu promulgated these teachings three centuries later after many years the Japanese Zen took these concepts and blended them with Buddhism. Today they have become the basis for many New Age cults.

Today we hear a lot about the negative and positive charge called the *Yin* and the *Yang*. The *Yang* is the positive force of good, life, light, summer (active) and masculinity. The *Yin* is the negative essence of evil, darkness, winter (passive), death and femininity. Some colleges teach courses called "The Tao of Physics," and take this view for scientific explanations. Even the "Star Wars" movies took on this concept of the good and bad side of "The Force." The symbol of *Yin* and *Yang* is a circle with a curved line dividing it. One side is black with a white dot and the other side white with a black dot.

Taoism appeals to those who have ecological concerns with the environment. If the *Yin* and the *Yang* were in balance, then there would be harmony on our earth. Men should live passively, avoiding all forms of stress and violence to properly commune with nature. In doing this, his life will flow with the Tao.[10]

Taoism is pantheistic and demonic because it hinges on magic. It has no solution for the cause of evil. Neither is there any scientific evidence for their beliefs. As a Christian, we know that evil comes from Satan and our flesh. Jesus said to take up our cross and follow Him (Mark 8:34). His yoke is easy and His burden light (Matthew 11:30). Taoism ignores problems of society, but Jesus tells us to evangelize others (Matthew 28:19) as well as providing for the stranger, the fatherless, and the widow (Deuteronomy 26:13).

ISLAM

Muhammad founded the origins of Islam around 570 A.D. in Mecca, Arabia. His parents died before he was six. A grandfather and an uncle raised him with whom he traveled extensively to Egypt and the Near East. Discussions with Jews and Christians influenced his teachings. At the age of 35 he married a 40 year-old wealthy women. She encouraged him to believe his visions.

Through life his views changed. He finally came to the belief that there was only one God, Allah. When he was 40, tradition tells us that he went into the Hira cave. Bob Larson writes in his book, *Larson's New Book of Cults,* the angel Gabriel supposedly appeared and choking him told him he must "proclaim in the name of the Lord the Creator who created man from a clot of blood" *(p.* 90-91). He returned to the cave often and wrote what he saw and heard in the sacred book now known as the *Koran (Quran,).* In Arabic *Koran* means "recitation."

The Koran was written in Arabic and contains prayers, rules of etiquette, and calls to "holy wars." Many of the beliefs come from the Bible and the historical foundation appear to come from the Old Testament. Because Mohammed was illiterate, he memorized 78,000 words (114 chapters) of his works.

The *Quran* also contains the Five Pillars of the Faith. Every Muslim who plans to escape judgment of Allah must do these things. One is to recite the *Shahada* ("There is no God but Allah, and Muhammad of the prophet of Allah"). Secondly they must bow toward Mecca five times a day and recite the prescribed prayer (*Salat* or *Namaz)* in Arabic. Thirdly, they must give alms (*Zakat)* and one-fortieth of their income. Fourthly, they must fast *(Saum* or *Ruzeh)* for the entire month of Ramadan. This is in atonement for sins of the past year. Lastly, they must make a pilgrimage *(Hajj)* to Mecca, their holy city, once in a lifetime.

When one witnesses to a Muslim, one must remember that they are very sincere about worshipping Allah. Their belief is that "There is no god but God, and Mohammed is the Messenger of God." This confession of faith is called *Shahada*, or one who submits. They do not believe in a personal God like Jesus is to the Christian. The concept that, "God so loved the world that He gave His only begotten Son," is very alien to their way of thinking. Their Allah is merciful, omniscient, and compassionate but he is held in such high awe that he is unapproachable. To them he is also a God of judgment, instead of grace mercy, and power. Thus their god is to be feared and strictly obeyed. They cannot fathom that God would personally care for them. Instead Allah's supreme attribute of justice overrules the love of God.

In Islam they believe in angels, especially since the angel Gabriel had visited Muhammad. Their Jinn (angel) is supposed to be a messenger of inspiration. We know the Bible speaks very clearly about devils, as it was Satan who was responsible for the fall of Adam and Eve (Genesis Chapter 3). Believing also that every person has angels who records good deeds and bad deeds. We know from the Bible that God gives angels instructions to watch over us and protect us. Psalm 91:11,12a says it clearly; "For He shall give His angels charge over you, to keep you in all your ways. In their hands they shall bear you up."

Muslims believe in four inspired books. The first book is the *Torah* or the book of Moses, the second book is the Psalms *(Zabin)*, which is of David, the third book is the Gospel of Christ called the *(Injil)*, and the last book is their *Quran*. Since the *Quran* was written last, they believe it is the final word to man and is more important than the rest.

The Muslims also believe that the first three books corrupted the Christians and the Jews.

Muslims also believe that Jesus was a great prophet and not the Son of God. When witnessing to them we can give them the scripture in John 3:16 which discounts this belief for it says, "For God so loved the world that He gave His only begotten Son, that whoever believes in Him should not perish but have everlasting life." Along with Jesus, Muslims consider Adam, Noah, Abraham, Moses and Muhammad to be prophets. They feel that Muhammad is the greatest of them all.

While watching Trinity Broadcasting Network, I heard Dr. Paul Crouch read from the *Quran* . It clearly stated that they believe in the virgin birth. According to the gentleman who had been a Muslim and was being interview by Mr. Crouch, told him that most Muslims do not read the *Quran*. If most Moslems would read the *Quran* there would be greater understanding among Christians and Moslems. They also would more easily come to the truth of Jesus Christ as Lord and not be deceived by the enemy.

Regarding eternity, Muslims believe that if they obey, and follow Allah and Muhammad they will go to an Islamic Paradise or a place of pleasure. They believe that those who do not agree with the Muslims will go to hell. We can share with them from Ephesians 2:8-9, "For by grace you have been saved through faith, and that not of yourselves; it is the gift of God, not of works, lest anyone should boast." Salvation does not depend on works but the love of God and belief in Jesus.

Chapter X

Western Religions

EDGAR CAYCE
(ASSOCIATION FOR RESEARCH
AND ENLIGHTENMENT)

Edgar Cayce was born in 1877 and died in 1945. He used Numbers 12:6 to back his claim that he was the "sleeping prophet." It says, "Then He said, 'Hear now My words: If there is a prophet among you, I, the LORD, make Myself known to him in a vision; I speak to him in a dream.'"

During Edgar's childhood a Mormon lady who believed in reincarnation lived with the family. She believed she had been married to Bringham Young in an earlier life. Mr. Young was a Mormon who believed in reincarnation. This may be where Cayce learned reincarnation. Reincarnation became a major part of his belief system.

Cayce blamed the third century translators for omitting reincarnation from the church canon. Reincarnation was an excuse to justify any sexual perversion. In one of his publications called *Many Mansions,* it says homosexuality is the result of a psychological imprint from a former life.

When Cayce was 13 years of age, he had an apparition of a woman and she offered to grant him any request. He stated that he wanted to help sick people, and she granted him his wish. He was using an incorrect spirit guide. This was not the Holy Spirit.

Several family members exhibited psychic ability. His grandfather did water witching. His father had power over snakes, could make tables move and brooms dance. Edgar having only a grade school education could sleep on a book and by morning knew and remembered the contents of the entire book.

When Cayce was 24 years of age, he lost his voice. No one could cure him. During a deep hypnotic trance his voice came back. A. C. Layne, the hypnotist suggested Cayce help others the same way. Cayce became a successful hypnotist. Layne suggested Cayce had a clairvoyant gift (unusually perceptive or discerning, also one who possesses power of discerning, objects not present to the senses) (Webster p. 152). This gift was called "readings." Cayce would use this gift to read peoples physical and emotional problems then give solutions for a cure. He was very successful through his readings. In his life he had over 16,000 readings in which he could help others who were suffering.

Cayce believed this was the result of the request he made from the woman who appeared to him and he claimed the gift to be God given. This was how he rationalized his psychic ability. During this time he continued to teach Sunday school and claimed that his psychic ability was God-given.

When Cayce was 56, he met Arthur Lammers. Lammers was involved in Theosophy. Webster defines theosophy as:

1. A belief about God and the world to be based on mystical insight,
2. The beliefs of a modern movement originating

in the U.S. in 1875 and followed chiefly Buddhist and Bramanic theories especially of pantheistic, evolution and reincarnation and occultism (p.916).

Arthur encouraged Edgar Cayce to continue with his readings in which he received cures for the mind and the body by his altered state of consciousness. Cayces claim to be a prophet has no scriptural basis. Most of his readings and utterances speak of spiritism. Neither did the claims to be a prophet line up with the word of God as in Deuteronomy 18:20-22 " 'But the prophet who presumes to speak a word in My name which I have not commanded him to speak, or who speaks in the name of other gods, that prophet shall die'. And if you say in your heart, 'How shall we know the word which the LORD has spoken?'— when a prophet speaks in the name of the LORD, if the thing does not happen or come to pass, that is the thing which the LORD has not spoken; the prophet has spoken it presumptuously; you shall not be afraid of him." We can see from this he took the scripture to make it fit his situation. He was not speaking for God but under the influence of a demonic spirit.

There are several ways the enemy led Edgar Cayce astray. First, he was under generational curses. Exodus 20:5-6 states, "You shall not bow down to them nor serve them. For I the LORD your God, am a jealous God, visiting the iniquity of the fathers upon the children to the third and fourth generations of those who hate Me, but showing mercy to thousands, to those who love Me and keep My commandments." His father, mother, and grandfather were all involved in cultic practices.

Secondly, when one evaluates Cayce's life, one would say that he had a strong call on his life to serve the Lord. God was drawing him through reading the Bible. Since the devil has been around over 6000 years, he knows how certain people are living and how God may be drawing them. The enemy will do anything to cheat, kill and destroy a person (John 10:10). In Edgar's case the enemy deceived his mind so he could not have the mind of Christ and follow his calling for the Lord.

Thirdly, if Cayce knew the Word well enough, the woman who appeared to him would not have deceived him. Hosea 4:6 states, "My people are destroyed for lack of knowledge. Because you have rejected knowledge, I also will reject you from being priest for Me: because you have forgotten the law of your God, I also will forget your children." Since the devil comes like an angel of light (2 Corinthians 11:14), apparently Cayce thought the woman was sent from God. When apparitions happen whether it is a person or an angel; one needs to ask them if they serve the Lord Jesus Christ? If they disappear one will know they are not from God. This is one way to test the spirits as the word confirms in 1 John 4:1, "Beloved, do not believe every spirit, but test the spirits, whether they are of God; because many false prophets have gone out into the world."

Fourthly I am convinced that Mr. Cayce had never received salvation. Even though he had knowledge of the Bible, but did not have the light of Jesus in him, he could not discern the Word correctly. The scripture in 1 Corinthians 2:14-16 says, "But the natural man does not receive the things of the Spirit of God, for they are foolishness to him; nor can he know them, because they are spiritually discerned. But he who is spiritual judges all things, yet he himself is rightly judged by no one. For who has known the mind of the LORD that he may instruct him? But we have the mind of Christ." I'm sure that if Cayce had been saved he would have recognized the apparition as not coming from God. One would think that Cayce would have had enough truth of the Word in him after teaching Sunday School, to be able to discern he was being deceived.

One time Dwight L. Moody, an evangelist, was in Cayce's area and Edgar shared with him about having visions and hearing voices. Rev. Moody warned him that evil spirits could be doing this. I believe the reason Cayce did not heed the warning is because the Word of God states that the carnal mind cannot understand the things of the Spirit. The erroneous teaching of Layne, Cayce exposure to theory of reincarnation and after Lammers encouraged him go to on with his "readings," Cayce severely departed from all biblical truth. He was dabbling is the world of darkness. Jesus the Light of this world dispels darkness!

MORMONISM

Mormonism is a religion that is also called the Church of the Latter Day Saints. They believe in their prophet Joseph Smith. In their *Doctrine of Salvation*, (Vol. 1, p. 189), they believe there is no salvation without accepting Joseph Smith. Since the beginning of Mormonism there has been over 100 variations of this religion. For example, some believe in polygamy and others do not. Their membership is over 5,500,000 and their income annual budget is in the billions.

Joseph Smith's mother was involved in the occult and she had visions. His father was a treasure seeker digging up the "fabled booty" of Captain Kidd. Joseph Jr. went with his father on these expeditions. He became involved in divination, and fortune telling by "peep stones" for money. The "peep stones" were considered magical stones. When the stone or stones were placed in a hat and in a dark area, they would reveal buried treasures. Joseph Smith Jr. was arrested for adultery, murder, and destroying the "Nauvoo Expositor Newspaper" press. In *The Kingdom of the Cults*, Walter Martin reported that "peep stone" gazing was one of several occult practices that were illegal in the 1820s. At Mr. Smith's death in jail they found this "glass looking stone" on his person. Joseph Smith was tried and found guilty of the "peeping stone" practice in Norwich, New York in 1826 (p.186).

One can easily conclude that he had strong cultic ties. He was also involved in Masonry, which influenced his beliefs and opened his soul up to satanic influences, causing him to be easy prey for any demonic being or apparition that may appear.

Mr. Joseph Smith Jr. is believed to have had a vision of God the Father and Jesus Christ in 1820. With this vision and others that followed, it was revealed to him that other religions were an "abomination unto the Lord" and Joseph was to restore the true gospel. Private revelation is never to take the place of the written inspired Word of God (2 Timothy 3:16).

Three years after the vision the angel Morani appeared at Joseph's bedside. Morani said he was the son of Mormon, who had been a leader of an American race called "Nephites Morone." He told him about the buried golden plates in the hill Cumorah near Palmyra, New York and these plates were to contain "the fullness of the everlasting Gospel." This was a deceptive tactic of Satan. Most of the information on the plates was in direct contradiction to the Bible. The teaching of Morone is a contradiction from the gospel what Paul refers to in Galatians 1:8-9. Paul states, "But even if we, or an angel from heaven, preach any other gospel to you than what we have preached to you, let him be accursed."

Mormons believe the Bible is flawed and inferior to Joseph Smiths words. The last chapter of the Book of Revelation 22:18 says, "For I testify to everyone who hears the words of the prophecy of this book: if anyone adds to these things, God will add to him the plagues that are written in this book." From this we know Joseph Smith's beliefs are in error.

There are many heretical beliefs in the Mormon faith.

They believe that Jesus is the brother of Satan, Jesus was married to the sisters of Lazarus and to Mary Magdalene, Jesus' wives and children were present at His crucifixion, there is a mother and father in heaven, that God is not an eternal being but worked himself up to Godhood, and that Mormon men become gods of their own planets. As gods they can have millions of wives and enjoy much sex. Lastly their belief is that only those who are Mormons will be saved.[11] None of these beliefs line up with the Word of God.

An effective way to witness to Mormons is to pray first. They usually visit ones home by coming in pairs, are neatly dressed in white shirts with ties, and a dark suit. Their name badge will probably have the name "Elder" on it. Bob Larson says in his book, *Larson's New Book of Cults* that they are sincere beyond question. They represent the most basic of human values of patriotism, sobriety, familial responsibilities, and hard work (p. 308).

It is best not to invite them into our homes. If they offer to pray, suggest they let you pray and let them say what they came to say. They will want to give you the *Book of Mormons,* and explain that your "bosom will burn." This is how their Mormon spirit is transferred. If you ask them if the *Book of Mormons* has a familiar spirit, they will usually answer "yes." In case they do not know, tell them to ask their bishop or refer to *A Marvelous Work and a Wonder* (p. 67,68). One should refuse to accept their book or literature because of what Leviticus 19:31 says, "Give no regard to mediums and familiar spirits; do not seek after them, to be defiled by them: I am the LORD your God." Invite them to read Luke 24:13-32 about the disciples on the way to Emmaus. Verse 32 says, "And they said to one another, 'Did not our heart burn within us while He talked with us on the road, and while He opened the Scriptures to us?' " Because of this, one should choose to obey God in what He says in His Word.

Explain that the "burning in the bosom" is for believers who believe in Jesus Christ. Take them to John Chapter 3 and explain that even Nicodemus needed to be born again. This could be followed with ones personal testimony of finding Christ as Savior. If they leave, continue to pray that the Holy Spirit will convict them. Ask the Lord to send them the Spirit of Truth as in John 14:15 "If you love Me, keep my commandments. And I will pray the Father, and He will give you another Helper that He may abide with you forever—the Spirit of truth, whom the world cannot receive, because it neither sees Him nor knows Him; but you know Him, for He dwells with you and will be in you."

FREEMASONRY

Freemasonry is the ultimate of all secret orders and the most powerful in the world. Whenever there is secrecy, one can question it is perverse and deceitful. Usually it will have the name of a Lodge in front of it. If any thing is wonderful and good then it need not be kept secret.

Free Masons believe they can trace their origin to the building of Solomon's Temple. Yet even if it can be traced back that far, what would it prove? That belief does not give their doctrine any validy. Hiram Abiff, who was believed to be the builder of Solomon's Temple, was credited with being able to keep all his building ideas a secret. This is where the Masons get their name.

Freemasonry was revived in 1717 in Great Britain. Some of their religious, philosophical symbols and principles can be traced back to ancient sun worship. At this meeting in London, four lodges came into existence and the third degree of Masonry was adopted. Albert Pike (who helped lay down a lot of the rules and regulations) was involved with occult Luciferian ideas.

The Masons claim that Jesus, John the Baptist and John

the Evangelist were Masons. This is contrary to Jesus' words in John 18:20, where it says, "Jesus answered him, 'I spoke openly to the world, I always taught in synagogues and in the temple, where the Jews always meet, and in secret I have said nothing.' " Secret societies cannot make this claim.

Many politicians have been Masons. George Washington was only technically a Mason. He wrote to preacher Snyder, "That is, I presided over none, nor have I been in one more than once or twice within the last 30 years." Other presidents involved were Lyndon and Andrew Johnson, Polk, Buchanan, Garfield, McKinley, Roosevelt, and Taft who were last to join for political reasons. Several other presidents were against secret orders.

The Blue Lodge represents the first three Masonic Degrees, which are: Entered Apprentice, Fellowcraft, and Master Mason. When the Blue Lodge Members come into the Entered Apprentice, they take an oath. They are blindfolded, half dressed, kneel before an altar with a Bible, a square, a compass and then take oaths and agree to penalties. They pledge, "Binding myself under no less penalty than that of having my throat cut from ear to ear, my tongue torn out by its roots and buried in the sands of the sea, at low water mark, where the tide ebbs and flows twice in 24 hours, should I in the least knowingly, or wittingly violate or transgress this my Entered Apprentice obligation. So help me God and keep me steadfast."

The Master Mason says something similar. He pledges, "Binding myself under no less penalty than that of having my body severed in twain, my bowels taken from thence and burned to ashes, and this scattered by the four winds of heaven, that no more resemblance may be had among men or Mason of so vile a wretch as I should be, should I be the least, knowingly or wittingly violate or transgress this my Master Mason obligation, so help me God and keep me steadfast." Christians should not be making such pledges or oaths as they are contrary to scripture, blasphemous, profane, and emit an antichrist spirit.

Men in the order of Masonry have been known to murder. Due to their oaths they may not reveal anything about the crime or who committed the crime. The Honorable William L. Strong says, "The garments of Masonry are stained with blood." He was referring to the murder of Captain William Morgan years ago. No Mason would come forth even though they knew what had happened to Captain Morgan. In this case they did not stand up for truth. Jesus is the way the truth and the life (John 14:6).

Masonry is a religion according to Albert Mackey's, *Manuel of the Lodge,* (p. 215). Masons do not use the name of Jesus in their prayers. In the Mark Master Degree which is the first degree above the Blue Lodge, they refer to 1 Peter 2:5 and leave out the name of Jesus. They do the same thing in the Royal Arch (7th degree), of the York Rite, and four degrees of Chapter Masonry when they quote 2 Thessalonians 3:6-16. Again they leave out the name of Christ.

Jesus says in John 14:6, "I am the way, the truth, and the life. No one comes to the Father except through Me." In Mark 8:38 it says, "For whoever is ashamed of Me and My words in this adulterous and sinful generation, of him the Son of Man also will be ashamed when He comes in the glory of His Father with the holy angels."

Another reason Masonry is non-Christian is because it teaches the Universal Fatherhood of God and the Brotherhood of Man as their underlying principles. Jesus is only a man and a teacher, they answer only to a Supreme Being. George Thornburg wrote about this in his *History of Masonry* on page 41. He made it very clear that the Masons believed in the Fatherhood of God and the Brotherhood of Man without Jesus. The Scripture in Galatians 3:26 disproves what the Masons believe which says, "For you are all sons of God through faith in Christ Jesus."

Masonry is against the Bible because it teaches salvation by works and character. When someone enters the Entered Apprentice they receive a white apron from the Master of the Lodge as he says, "You are presented with a lambskin or white apron because the lamb has in all ages been deemed an emblem of innocence. He therefore, who wears the lambskin or white leather apron as the badge of a Mason, is thereby continually reminded of that purity of conduct which is essentially necessary to his gaining admission into the Celestial Lodge above, where the Supreme Architect of the Universe presides." Ephesians 2:8-9 says, "For by grace you have been saved through faith, and that not of yourselves; it is the gift of God, not of works, lest anyone should boast." From these verses one understands that salvation and thus entrance into heaven, is purely a gift by faith in Jesus and not by works.

Masonry is fashioned after heathen practices and ancient sun-worshippers. Albert Mackey who wrote the *Encyclopedia of Free Masonry,* says in his other book, *Ritualist,* (p.112) "The idea of the legend was undoubtedly borrowed from Ancient Mysteries." He was referring to the legend of Hiram Abiff (builder of Solomon's Temple), which is enacted in the third degree of Masonry. In Mackey's *Lexicon,* speaks of the Ancient Mysteries as "truly Masonic Institutions." Mackey also says in the same book, (p. 353) that in their Masonic symbol the point within the circle, was borrowed from heathen sun worship. He states that the symbol was adopted by the idolatrous Israelites, who took if from the Moabites in the wilderness of Sin, under the name of Baal-Peor." According to the First Commandment given to Moses, God's judgment came on the Israelites when they engaged in Baal Worship.

"The religion of Free Masonry is not Christianity," says Albert Mackey's in the *Encyclopedia of Freemasonry,* (p. 618-619). If it is not Christianity, then it is not of God. Read in Galatians 1:8 where it says, "But even if we, or an angel from heaven, preach any other gospel to you than what we have preached to you, let him be accursed. As we have said before, so now I say again, if anyone preaches any other gospel to you than what you have received, let him be accursed." According to this passage, any gospel other that the Gospel of Jesus Christ will be cursed.

The Masonic symbols are the white apron, representing the innocence of the Lamb, is worn at meetings, and Masons are buried in the apron. The star and the five points of fellowship represent the 3rd degree Mason. The Beehive denotes fertility of Queen Bee and there is also the all Seeing Eye of Horus. On their ring is a compass and square with a "G" which means a god deity. These are not Christian symbols.

Shriners are the highest degree of Masons. They have the Eastern Star for women Masons, the Order of DeMolay for teenage boys, and the Order of the Rainbow for teenage girls. The Masons are all philanthropic. They do many good works, supporting widows, nursing homes, and 22 Shiner hospitals for cripple children. However, in Ephesians 2:9 Paul says, "not of works, lest anyone should boast." Again, it is by faith in Jesus alone that we are saved.

People join the Masons for social status and to help others. Many Masons do not know what Christianity teaches. Others never delve into what Masonry is either. Some professing Christians belong because they have denied the Deity of Christ and His blood atonement. 2 Corinthians 6:14-18, "Do not be unequally yoked together with unbelievers. For what fellowship has righteousness with lawlessness? And what communion has light with darkness? And what accord has Christ with Belial? Or what part has a believer with an unbeliever? And what agreement has the temple of God with idols? For you are the temple of the living God. As God has said: 'I will dwell in them and walk among them. I will be their God, and they shall be my people'. Therefore 'Come out from among them and be separate, says the Lord. Do not touch what is unclean, and I will receive you.' 'I will be a Father to you, And you shall be My sons and daughters, says the LORD Almighty.' " Again God's word speaks for itself.

JEHOVAH'S WITNESS AND TRACT SOCIETY

Charles Taze Russell (born 1852) began the Jehovah's Witness religion. It is also known as the Tract Society and Watchtower Bible. When Mr. Russell was eighteen, he began a Bible class and the members of his class gave him the title of Pastor. Mr. Russell had only a seventh-grade education and no formal theological training. He was never ordained as a minister. Ten years later he left Orthodox Christianity and began denying the existence of hell, the deity of Christ, and the belief in the Trinity. In an effort to reach more people, he published his teachings in *The Herald of the Morning* magazine with its cofounder N. H. Barbour. By the time Mr. Russell was forty-two, he controlled the publication, and renamed it, *The Watchtower Announing Jehovah's Kingdom*. He later founded, *The Watchtower* magazine. In the beginning the Jehovah's Witnesses published 6,000 copies annually and today they put out 800,000 daily.

After Mr. Russell's death, Joseph Franklin Rutherford, a Missouri lawyer, became president of the Jehovah's. Like Mr. Russell, he alone had complete authority over the organization. At the convention in Columbus, Ohio in 1931, Mr. Rutherford changed the name of the organization to Jehovah's Witnesses. Until this time the Jehovah's did not have a specific name. He uses the scripture in Isaiah 43:10a,b, "You are My witnesses, 'says the LORD, and My servant whom I have chosen'." The name was changed in an effort to cover up Mr. Russell's damaging background and convince the people the Jehovah's Witness was a new organization.

After Mr. Rutherford's death, Nathan Knorr became the

autocratic leader of the Witnesses. Today an elderly man, Fredrick Wilham Franz has the power and authority over the organization. Because of the autocratic power the members may not deviate from their strict rules, beliefs or even question their doctrine. To question or disagree with anything would cause them to be disfellowshipped (excommunicated). Those excommunicated are told they will not rise on Judgment Day and even relatives are not to speak to them and treat them as if they were dead. Any member found reading material written by ex-members were to be shunned, and are not to eat with anyone who might be a dissenter.

The Jehovah's Witness do not believe in the Word of God for the doctrine of the Trinity of the Godhead. They believe God is a solitary being from eternity, unequaled, unrevealed, and unknown. Jehovah to them is the almighty and supreme sovereign of the universe and not omnipresent, but with power extending everywhere. The Jehovah's Witness belief contradicts scripture which states in 1 John 5:7, "For there are three that bear witness in heaven: the Father, the Word, and the Holy Spirit; and these three are one."

The Jehovah's Witnesses believe that Jesus was born as a human son of God and the first creation by His Father Jehovah. Jesus was God's vindicator and the Chief Agent of life for man. He became the Messiah, died on a stake for our ransom, was resurrected immortal on the third day and His body did not corrupt. They cannot explain what happened to the body. Mr. Rutherford wrote in *The Kingdom Is At Hand* that Jesus is not equal to Jehovah God but was Michael the Archangel in his preexistent state, having a brother named Lucifer who rebelled against God while Michael remained obedient to God (p.49). In Colossians 1:15 it calls Jesus the firstborn. The Jehovah's Witnesses interpret the Bible to mean the first created. Jesus is God and not a creation. If they read on in verse 17 it states, "And He is before all things, and in Him all things consist." This scripture contradicts their belief.

Any organization that denies the deity of Christ is a cult.

As part of their belief system, they refuse to permit their members to receive blood transfusions. They quote Genesis 9:4, "But you shall not eat flesh with its life, that is, its blood" and also Leviticus 17:12, "Therefore I said to the children of Israel, 'No one among you shall eat blood, nor shall any stranger who dwells among you eat blood.'" If they receive a blood transfusion it is considered to be the same thing as eating it. Neither do they allow organ transplants, members may not serve in the armed forces, salute, pledge to any flag, sing national songs as "The Star Spangle Banner," vote, and may not observe any Christian, cultural or national holidays as they are considered idolatrous. Any member observing the holidays will be disfellowshipped.

The Jehovah's Witnesses believe the Holy Spirit is an invisible active force from God that moves God's people to do His will. According to 1 John 5:7 this is an erroneous opinion as the Father, Word, and Holy Spirit are equal. From John 14:26 we know He came to teach us everything including the truth, "But the Helper, the Holy Spirit, whom the Father will send in My name, He will teach you all things, and bring to your remembrance all things that I said to you." The Holy Spirit is not only God, but also He dwells in us (Roman 8:11).

They also believe the eating of the forbidden fruit in the Garden of Eden by Adam and Eve brought death to mankind. Man is a soul and is not separate from the body, and upon mans death there is no soul consciousness but an unconscious annihilation to the dust in the earth. According to their belief Adam was not sent to eternal torment, but to the unconscious annihilation. As Christians we are all sinners including Adam and Eve and only in Jesus do we have redemption through His blood and forgiveness of our sins (Ephesians 1:7). We have a spiritual body that will be raised. This is clarified in 1 Corinthians 15:44, "It is sown a natural body, it is raised a spiritual body. There is a natural body, and there is a spiritual body." The scripture goes on to say in verse 51, "Behold, I tell you a mystery: we shall not all sleep, but we shall all be changed." This passage does not refer to unconscious annihilation. When a belief system does not line up with the word of God, it is not true doctrine.

Door to door evangelism or "preaching" as they call it, is considered necessary for Witnesses to be saved. They must participate in "Bible" studies, which are Watchtower doctrines and practices required for their spiritual growth. According to the Watchtower statistics on the Internet for the year 2000, they spent over 1.1 billion hours "preaching" door to door and shared in more than 4.7 million "Bible" studies worldwide. The countries with the most congregations are the United States, Mexico, Brazil, and Nigeria.

Another service of the Jehovah's Witness is the Lord's Supper. There is an annual unbiblical "Memorial of Christ's Death at Passover" service celebrated by a minority of the members classified as "anointed" or "spiritual class" who receive bread and wine. Only those born before 1914 come in this class as the number of 144,000, were filled by then. It is believed there are only about 9,000 to 10,000 "anointed" ones left.

The Jehovah's Witness take the number of 144,000 literally from Revelations 7:4. They consider themselves to be spiritual Israelites. The Gentile era ended with the sealing of 144,000 who would be priests and kings in heaven. This will happen after the battle of Armageddon and they are eager for it to begin. Those born after 1914 would be a servant class and can look forward to living eternally on a perfected earth.

The Watchtower and Tract Society published their own Bible in 1961 called, *New World Translation of the Holy Scriptures.* In the forward of their Bible it states, "The Son of God taught the traditions of creed-bound men that made the commandments and teachings of God of no power and effect.

The endeavor of the New World Bible Translation committee has been to avoid this sort of religious traditionalism." The Jehovah's Witness have attempted to prove their unbiblical teaching by editing it. By changing the word of God and doing their own unbiblical teaching is contrary to what the word of God says in the Book of Revelation 22:18,19, "For I testify to everyone who hears the words of the prophecy of this book: if anyone adds to these things, God will add to him the plagues that are written in this book; and if anyone takes away from the words of the book of prophecy, God shall take away his part from the Book of Life, from the holy city, and from the things which are written in this book."

The headquarters of the Jehovah's Witness is in Brooklyn, New York. It is a huge complex run by volunteers who receive housing, bare necessities, and extremely minimum wages for personal expenses. The "heavenly class" or "anointed men" of twelve that make up the governing board runs the headquarters. They are the only ones they believe have the authority to understand and teach their Bible.

UNITY

Charles and Myrtle Fillmore the founders of the Unity church (1889) came from a background of various religious experiences. Myrtle was raised a Methodist, Charles dabbled in Spiritualism and both were influenced by Mrs. Eddy of the Christian Science religion. When they left Christian Science, they changed the name of their cult to Unity. Following the other religious experiences, they drifted in the "New Thought." Their last religious influence came from a Yoga Master, Swami Vivekananda of India. Because of all these influences, their belief system was anything but Christian. Neither of them had any contact with Christianity.

The Fillmores claimed many personal healings. Myrtle was healed of tuberculosis. The healings led to the founding of the Society of Silent Health known today as the Society of Silent Unity. Credit for healings are given to an abstract deity and what Myrtle called "the love principles as taught by Christ" which was published in *Modern Thought,* (Vol. 1, October 1889, No. 80). Each year they receive nearly 2.5 million requests for help. The Silent Unity solves people's problems also by encouraging positive thinking. Research shows that a positive outlook on life is therapeutic physically, emotionally and helps in the healing process.

The Unity church does not believe in sin. Unity calls sin falling short of our divine nature and forgiveness is to erase out thoughts from being conscience of sin. After removing the illusion of sin, there is suppose to be an inflow of divine love. It is by the thought process of the mind that man will be redeemed. Jesus is not deity and God is a principle, not a person. God is the love in everybody. The Holy Spirit is not recognized as the one who inspired the Bible. The Spirit merely reigns in the whole world.

Every one of these teachings is contrary to the Bible. God is not a principle He is our creator. It is stated in Isaiah 40:28, "Have you not known? Have you not heard? The everlasting God, the LORD, the Creator of the ends of the earth, neither faints nor is weary. His understanding is unsearchable." Jesus is Lord as stated in Philippians 2:11, "and that every tongue should confess that Jesus Christ is LORD, to the glory of God the Father." The Holy Spirit did inspire the written word of God in 2 Timothy 3:16, "All Scripture is given by inspiration of God, and is profitable for doctrine, for reproof, for correction, for instruction in righteousness."

The Unity Church is a very fast growing church because of its love and harmony ideas. They seem to accept any new thing that comes down the pike. Rarely do they consult the Word of God; if they did they might come under the conviction of the Holy Spirit, "For the word of God is living and powerful, and sharper than any two-edged sword, piercing even to the division of soul and spirit, and of joints and marrow, and is a discerner of the thoughts and intents of the heart." (Hebrews 4:12)

THE UNIFICATION CHURCH

The founder of the Unification Church is Rev. Sun Myung Moon. It is better known as a New Age cult called the "Moonies" and is very visible with people who sell roses at the roadside. Rev. Moon was born in North Korea in 1920. He has fallen out of grace with Korea's governmental leaders because of his poor image.

He was put in Danbury Federal Correctional Institution because of a twelve-point indictment, one of which was for tax evasion. Upon discharge he served several months at the Brooklyn's Oxford Project Halfway House. During this time he was still conducting his church affairs and it seemed to appear he was above the law. The publicity caused the membership of the Unification Church to increase nearly six percent the next year.

Mose Durst, Moon's aide, claims Moon to be the "second Messiah" to succeed Jesus. Moon is to take up where Christ left off. Rev. Moon has many other bizarre ideas. To name a few, he denies the omnipotence of God, refers to the Holy Spirit as female, ridicules Christ's resurrection, the members can receive forgiveness of sin through works for Moon, denies salvation through Jesus, did "blood cleansing" to remove generational curses by female members having sex with Moon, he has done mass weddings of which Moon chose all the mates for all the couples, and the list goes on. None of these practices coincide with the practices in the Bible.

PART 4

Holistic Medicine

Chapter XI

The Enemy's Tactics in Alternative Medicine

We must know our enemy who is very subtle when it comes to holistic health and alternative medical methods of treatment. Satan has drawn certain people into the fields that are searching for the truth. Whether we know it or not, every one of us is searching for truth. Christians know the way of God is truth. The Father, Son, and Holy Spirit are one (1 John 5:7). The Father created the universe, including Adam and Eve (Genesis 1:31), the Son became man to redeem us from our sins and the sin of Adam and Eve, Jesus died for our sins (2 Corinthians 5:20), rose from the dead (1 Thessalonians 4:14), ascended into heaven (Ephesians 4:10), and sent us the Holy Spirit our helper (John 15:26).

Satan has taken the good things and counterfeited them for his purposes. He will use people as puppets to work through, especially people who are not knowledgeable about the truth. The puppets are deceived people we all need to be aware of so we are not also deceived.

Holistic health care is coming to the foreground more each day. With over 300 people dying each day in the United States from prescription drugs, having limited or no medical insurance; people are taking their health care in their own hands. Because of this, people are coming back to medical treatments used years ago, the use of herbs, essential oils, and nutritional supplements. These treatments may be good in themselves, but we must not let the enemy deceive us.

There is a difference in the terms between holistic and wholistic. Webster defines holistic as; 1: of or relating to holism and 2: emphasizing the organic or functional relation between parts (p.1019). Wholistic refers in medicine to the complete and total person. Including not only the body, but also the soul and spirit as well.

Recognizing the whole person was one of the key ingredients we were taught to be concerned about in nurses training. We were to be considerate about the spiritual aspect along with the bodily care. Most of the time we were so busy caring for the physical body that we forgot about the spiritual. Because of this I do not think we did a very good job of treating the whole person. This left the door open for the holistic health care approach we experience in some arenas today.

Holistic health care appears to be instigated by Satan himself. He sought to do this through a movement called "New Thought." The idea stemmed from the founders of Unity, by Charles and Myrtle Fillmore. Many of the practices of Unity were things such as palm reading, fortune telling, and handwriting analysis and also included Hindu teachings of reincarnation and karma. "New Thought" teaches that our consciousness is part of the great collection or cosmic consciousness: The Divine Mind, therefore, we are God."[12] Satan also wanted to be like God. In Ezekiel 28:1-2 it states, "The word of the LORD came to me again saying, 'Son of man, say to the prince of Tyre, 'Thus says the LORD GOD: Because your heart is lifted up, you say, I am a god, 'I sit in the seat of gods, In the midst of the seas', Yet you are a man, and not a god, Though you set your heart as the heart of a god." The "New Thought" has evolved into the New Age Movement. The idea of a movement, which Webster calls "The act or process of moving; especially: change of place or position or posture" (p.555). The New Age Movement has a goal of moving toward a one-world order. The god of a new world order is Satan himself. He wants to rule over the world. By becoming a god of this world he expects to be have authority and be worshipped. We are warned in 2 Thessalonians 2:3-4 which says, "Let no one deceive you by any means; for that Day will not come unless the falling away comes first, and the man of sin is revealed, the son of perdition, who opposes and exalts himself above all that is called God or that is worshipped, so that he sits as God in the temple of God, showing himself that he is God." One can see from the Word of God what Satan is up to.

Edgar Cayce is believed to be the father of Holistic Health. I have discussed before where his readings were not divinely inspired by God as he thought, but rather from Satan. Scripture tells us what to do in Ephesians 5:11-14, "And have no fellowship with the unfruitful works of darkness, but rather expose them. For it is shameful even to speak of those things, which are done by them in secret. But all things that are exposed are made manifest by the light. Therefore He says, 'Awake, you who sleep, Arise from the dead, and Christ will give you light.' " For us to have fellowship with the darkness of Satan opens one up to satanic influence. Rather than have fellowship, we should expose them for what they are.

Satan wanted equality with the Lord as in Isaiah 14:14, "I will ascend above the heights of the clouds, I will be like the Most High." He is behind every cult. Since he is the father of lies, he has attempted to deceive people ever since he deceived Eve in the Garden of Eden. He goes around seeking who he can devour. Holistic medicine has been influenced by New Age philosophy. Various aspects of alternative medicine have also been tinged by their humanistic approach. People perish for a lack of knowledge (Hosea 4:6). My purpose is to inform people about what has been sidestepped from the truth. The idea of wholistic medicine is the treatment of the total persons body, soul, and spirit (1 Thessalonians 5:23). Most wholistic doctors are medical doctors or doctors of osteopathy. They offer a wide range of conventional drugs or surgery as well as alternative treatments. They emphasize the care of the total person; give attention to diet and exercise, plus mental and emotional support. Good doctor-patient relationship is developed. Once this relationship is established, the patient should be able to discern by the Spirit if their attending physician is of the Lord or dabbling in the cultic treatments. If the later is the case, then a demonic spirit could be transferred during treatments rather than the Spirit of Christ. This is the bottom line when considering any type of alternative medical therapy.

IRIDOLOGY

Iridology is one of the most controversial alternative practices in modern medicine today. Many of the Christian writers compare it to palm reading. If the one doing the exam is not properly trained and interprets the reading of the iris by their own intuition, then I believe it is witchcraft like the reading of palms. One must know the philosophy and intent of the one doing the exam. It is not adequate to ask the practitioner their beliefs, but discern by the Sprit if they are telling the truth, as well as to know them by their fruits. In Matthew 7:20 Gods word says, "Therefore by their fruits you will know them." Seek to know from others if they bear fruit. If the practitioner does not, then have nothing to do with them as they could pass on a demonic spirit. "A good tree cannot bear bad fruit, nor can a bad tree bear good fruit." (Matthew 7:18).

Most critics I have read about say that ophthalmologists do not put any credibility in iridology exams. The reason eye doctors do not is because they are only interested in the treatment of the eyes. Iridology is a diagnostic test to determine failing or diseased systems in the body. It is not a treatment; it is merely an examination to help determine medical therapy.

The medical profession and religious critics call it demonic, quackery, or fraudulent. Dr. Bernard Jensen has studied iridology for over fifty years. He says, "Iridology is the science and practice that reveals inflammation, where located and in what stage it is manifesting. The iris reveals body constitutions, inherent weaknesses, levels of health and the transitions that take place in a person's body according to the way he lives...the iris represents a communication system capable of handling an amazing quality of information."[13] From Dr. Jensen's definition we can discern that it is diagnostic and he proves this scientifically. Again, the danger of having an iridology reading is in the person who is doing it. If there is no scientific training and the reader is merely using his own intuition, one would want to be very cautious. In case the reader was operating under occult powers, then we would be opening ourselves up to demonic influences. Once the door is opened to any demonic activity, it creates a spiritual atmosphere for further demonic infiltration. If we leave a door ajar in our home and we have a cat, the cat will immediately push the door open and come in. To stay free from demonic activity, we need to avoid exposure and keep the door closed at all times.

When I was in nurses training, the doctors would always

look at the eye to see if the eye was intact. If the eyeball was yellow it indicated there was a backup of bile into the blood stream. From this symptom the doctor would conclude there was a problem with the gall bladder, bile duct, or the liver itself. Various tests would follow to determine the nature of the condition. If the eye is the mirror of the soul, I believe the eye can also be the mirror of the body.

I know of several people who have been to an Iridologist to have an iris reading. It was for diagnostic problems and every one had received a correct diagnosis. With the invention of computer technology, iridology is becoming more scientific. Like I said before we must know the religious philosophy of the Iridologist and walk in the gift of discernment of the Spirit. If we do not have the gift of discerning of spirits, we may ask God for it. He gives gifts liberally. In 1 Corinthians 14:1 we are to desire spiritual gifts. Merely ask and you shall receive. We do not have gifts because we do ask.

ACUPUNCTURE

Acupuncture is another controversial alternative medical therapy. It is considered demonic because it follows the energy meridians of Taoism. Centuries ago Taoism discovered the use of electro stimulus in the body called meridians. This was before we discovered God placed meridians on the earth. Webster defines meridians as:

1. *obs:* the hour of noon: MIDDAY
2. a great circle of celestial sphere passing through its poles and the zenith of a given place,
3. a high point
4a: (1): a great circle on the surface of the earth passing through the poles and any given place.
   (2): the half of such a circle included between

poles
b: a representation of such a circle or half circle numbered for longitude on a map or globe.(p.530).

This is where the Toaists get their symbol of a circle with a curved line through the center and a dot on each half. God said in Hosea 4:6, "My people are destroyed for lack of knowledge. Because you have rejected knowledge, I also will reject you from being priest for Me; because you have forgotten the law of your God, I also will forget your children." I believe that for years we let the Toaists operate because we rejected knowledge and forgot about God's law, God permitted nonChristians or Satan's people such as the Toaists to use God's knowledge. I think it is time to take back what the enemy has taken.

Today we are researching acupuncture and understand the good coming from it. It has scientific validity because the meridians in the body are real as defined by Webster. As Christians we must take precautions and know who the operator is or else we fall into the same trap as we did with what was just stated about Iridology.

AYURVEDA

Ayurveda dates back 4000 years and is coming more prevalent today. The root word *ayur* means life and *veda* means knowledge. It is a science known as knowledge of life. Ayurveda encompasses a person's life of body, soul, and spirit. This sounds good on the surface.

Ayurveda believes every human being comes from a creation of cosmic consciousness as a male energy called *Purusha,* and female energy *Prakruti.* The *Prakruti* is believed to be the divine creative will and is considered to be a supreme intelligence. *Purusha* is passive consciousness with no part in creation. Since the *Prakruti* is supreme, we know this does not line up with the way God created the universe in the beginning and also God is always referred to in the Bible as "He." There is no other God and He is the Alpha and the Omega. It is confirmed in Isaiah 44:6, "Thus says the LORD, the King of Israel, and his Redeemer, the LORD of hosts: I am the First and I am the Last; besides Me there is no God."

Ayurveda believes that health in a body is a balance between the body, mind, and consciousness. Ayurevda claims three *Doshas* namely: *Vata,* (ether and air), *Pitta* (fire and water), and *Kapha* (water and earth). Every cell and organ in the body is made up of all three *Doshas,* which is determined at birth. Disease can come from an imbalance from any of these.

Ayurveda is sometimes used in the diagnosis of a disease such as the tongue diagnosis, which reveals the functional status of body organs by looking at the surface of the tongue. If a disease is found in the body, Ayruveda believes the body has the intelligence to bring the body back into balance. The body can be helped to come back into balance by exercise, the use of herbs, dietary changes, body cleansing, meditation and massage. All of these treatments are not bad in themselves. Usually the exercise recommended is Yoga in which every movement is an act of worship to Satan. Transcendental Meditation places one into a subliminal state giving entry to Satanic oppression. The body or self-god is at the center of Ayruveda healing which is self-idolatry. This contradicts what God says in Exodus 20:2,3, "I am the LORD your God, who brought you out of the land of Egypt, out of the house of bondage. You shall have no other Gods before Me." Any time a medical practitioner has an Ayruveda background, one ought to be cautious.

AURAS

Reading of auras of a person must be understood with caution. The medical person with psychic ability gets this confused with the anointed glory of the Lord. Medical personnel who read auras around a person believe it is a manifestation of the higher self and is used to diagnose a medical problem. The reader sees an illumination of different colors depicting the emotional, spiritual, and physical state of the individual being read. A small aura of a few inches around the body displays tension, and an aura of several feet refers to a peaceful state of the individual being read.

If a non-Christian medical person has the psychic ability to see an aura around a person, I believe it is by the psychic power of Satan. Satan uses everything given by God and counterfeits it. He wants to receive God's glory for himself, as Satan wanted to be like God. He also has great knowledge as confirmed in Proverbs 29:13, "The poor man and the oppressor have this in common: the Lord gives light to the eyes of both."

I believe Satan is trying to counterfeit the glory of the Lord. He uses some people to do the reading as his pawns because they do not know they are to minister under the anointing of the Holy Spirit. God wants all his people to be saved (2 Peter 3:9), and walk in His power and glory (Acts 1:8). God gives some people an extra anointing power such as Benny Hinn, a TV Evangelist who walks in a healing anointing. Ezekiel saw God's glory in 3:23, "So I arose and went out into the plain, and behold, the glory of the LORD stood there, like the glory which I saw by the River Chebar; and I fell on my face." Every Christian has the ability to walk in the power of the anointing of the Holy Spirit.

Christians should not have aura readings done for medical conditions by a non-Christian or one who uses psychic power of the enemy. It is best to have an anointed person pray over you who has the gift of healing as stated in 1 Corinthians 12:9, "To another faith by the same Spirit, to another gifts of healings by the same Spirit," and one who walks in the anointing. The Holy Spirit can reveal what the persons problem is for God's word says in 1 John 2:20, "But you have an anointing from the Holy One, and you know all things." Associated with this prayer is the word of knowledge given by God as in 1 Corinthians 12:8, "For to one is given the word of wisdom through the Spirit, to another the word of knowledge through the same Spirit."

The anointing of the Anointed One in us flows into the person being prayed for. The Anointed One in us is confirmed in 2 Corinthians 1:21, "Now He who establishes us with you in Christ and has anointed us is God." No one needs to seek the help of others who use their energy to heal or read auras. Neither should we let non-Christians lay hands on us for healing as they can be transferring a demonic spirit and not the anointing of the Spirit of God. We know from scripture that healing takes place from the laying on of hands when Jairus went to Jesus, "and begged Him earnestly, saying, 'My little daughter lies at the point of death. Come and lay Your hands on her, that she may be healed, and she will live.'" (Mark 5:23).

PART 5

Influences On Children
And Youth

Chapter XII

Dangers of Fantasy Games

DUNGEONS AND DRAGONS

Dungeons and Dragons is a fantasy role-playing game. It involves characters from medieval mythology using terms like wizard, dragons, necromancer, sorcerer and the like. A Master, who is an expert player, leads the characters on a fantasy occult adventure through dragon filled dungeons, and controls the Dungeon Master. He battles evil warriors and scoops up treasures. During the game the players learn to cast spells, curses and they learn the technique of making magic potions.

The end goal of the game is to become a god. This is also the tactic of the New Age Movement. Satan uses this tactic to pull people away from God by opening their minds up through occult practices. It not only teaches them witchcraft but overt practices such as sacrificing animals and eventually satanic rituals as well.

Dungeons and Dragons is more than a mere fantasy game of dice and medieval characters. There is now a complete line of occult paraphernalia, books, toys, posters, membership cards, playing aids and even an annual player's convention. It appeals to people ages ten to twenty four years of age. At one time four million Americans were playing the game. Even though it was introduced in the seventies, its popularity grew rapidly in the eighties. Today it still influences many.

The consequences of Dungeons and Dragons cause some youth to commit suicide. Paul Vick, Director of Outreach Programs for "Association to Rescue Kids," gave several examples of boys committing suicide. Jeffrey Jacklovich, 14, from Kansas shot himself. Next to his body they found a note bequeathing the game of Dungeons and Dragons to his best friend.

Another teenager from Virginia committed suicide after his father refused to let him stay after school to play the game of Dungeon and Dragons. He left a note indicating that he believed he could resurrect himself. This deception came from the influence of the game.

Sometimes the players identify with their characters so closely they cross over the line between fantasy and reality. Even an innocent involvement in the game that glamorizes Satan and makes the Biblical account of hell a fantasy is dabbling in rebellion to Scripture and is forbidden in Deuteronomy 18:9-12. The Dungeon in the Bible (Revelations 9:1-2) is hell and the Dragon in the Bible is Satan (Revelations 12:7-9). Dungeons and Dragons is more than an innocent game!

POKEMON CARDS

The craze today for our people young people is the Pokemon Cards. The word Pokemon in Japanese is a slang term for "Pocket Monster." In 1998 Nintendo brought Pokemon from Japan to the United States in the form of cards, cartoons, toys, and video games. In February of 2000 the sale of Pokemon products were over one billion dollars. The Wizards of the Coast make the Pokemon Cards, which is the same company that made Dungeons and Dragons.

Children love to collect all 151 cards. This causes them to purchase additional booster packs that may or may not have a coveted card. As a result the kids began trading lunches, stealing, and even use force to obtain a specific card for their set. On December 8, 1999, the 700 Club reported that two boys from California (ages 12 and 13), were arrested for stealing cards from other students' backpacks. In New York another boy is recovering from stabbing over the Pokemon Cards (N324). The desire to possess these cards is so strong; most children seem to be obsessed with them.

Some of the cards have a satanic symbol of the extended thumb, index finger, and pinky. Another card emits special alpha waves from its body causing headaches to those near by. *Pokemon 65 Alakozan,* is believed to have super psychic ability. Each card has its own distinct personality and special powers. The belief systems of the Pokemon are influenced by Eastern Mystic Religions, which are also in Japan.

Trading the cards causes competition. Many children cannot afford the cards. They feel left out or unimportant because they cannot possess the cards. It puts a wedge between friends and ends up hurting their relationships. It creates greed, strife, combativeness and obsession. Some actually use the cards to put curses on each other or their parents.

A mother brought her eleven year-old boy to our home. All her four boys were hooked on the Pokemon Cards. They were constantly fighting, trading, and bickering over these cards. She took the cards away from them, but the one boy was brought to our home would not give them up. This lad opened his collection in front of me and an evil force emitted from them. I quickly covered us with the blood of Jesus and anointed the cards with oil and cast out any evil spirit. This made quite an impression on the lad. It was enough to convince him that the cards were evil. He agreed to go home and burn them. A few days later his mother called and said their home is so calm and peaceful again. She knew the cards were evil, but did not realize the extent of their influence.

HARRY POTTER'S BOOKS

There is a series of books called Harry Potter. Mrs. J. K. Rowling the author, was interviewed by *Newsweek* Magazine (July 17, 2000), and her comments were, "In fact, death and bereavement and what death means, I would say, is one of the central themes in all seven books"(p.56). Her books cover things of the occult in a fantasy way. Some books deal with sorcery (the use of power gained from the assistance or control of evil spirits), witchcraft, human and animal sacrifices, and the divine. The books have an overtone of sadness, death, hate, loss, and show lack of respect for others. There are tendencies toward evil, by casting spells, and doing incantations, entering the spirit world and becoming demon possessed.

John Andrew Murray wrote in *Teachers In Focus* magazine web site maintained by Focus on the Family an article entitled "Harry Dilemma." He commented, "But it is the world of witchcraft found in Harry Potter that is the greatest threat of all. This world—which will soon be a massive scale—is presenting occult practices in a way that is attractive and fun. And while few students are seeking to become witches or wizards, the desensitization to witchcraft that is occurring in America can not help but have a detrimental effect—and lead to serious spiritual consequences in the future." He goes on to say, "By disassociating magic and supernatural evil, it becomes possible to portray occult practices as 'good' and 'healthy', contrary to the scriptural declaration that such practices are 'detestable to the Lord'. This, in turn, opens the door for kids to become fascinated with the supernatural while tragically failing to seek or recognize the one true source of supernatural good—namely God. The problem with the Harry Potter series is the presentation of evil in an attractive, 'wholesome' package."

In Mrs. Rowling's book *The Sorcer's Stone,* refers to reincarnation and makes light of death. A professor tells Harry Potter, "After all to the well organized mind, death is but the next great adventure" (p.302). In her third book *The Prisoner of Azkaban,* she writes, "You can exist without your soul, you know, as long as your brain and heart are still working. But you'll have no sense of self anymore, no memory no ...anything. There's no chance at all of recovery. You'll just-exist. As an empty shell." (p.247). Our Bible tells us something different in Ecclesiastes 12:7, "Then the dust will return to the earth as it was, and the Spirit will return to God who gave it."

I actually had one parent tell me these books were merely a child's fantasy book like *Goldilocks and the Three Bears!* This is not childhood fantasy but the real dark world of Satan. We are to have nothing to do with seeds of darkness. The Word clearly tells us we cannot be a Christian and dabble in the things of Satan. "You cannot drink the cup of the Lord and the cup of demons; you cannot partake of the Lord's table and the table of demons" (1 Corinthians 10:21).

MAGIC GAME

Two or more players can play the Magic Game. There are approximately 3000 cards in the deck. The object of the game is that a powerful wizard tries to gain control of a magical place. The players can actually summon supernatural power to achieve their purpose. The cards can lead to casting spells on others or even become demon possessed by asking the spirits to enter them to give them power. The very word magic according to Webster means the use of means (as charms, spells) believed to have supernatural powers over natural forces (p.508). This definition alone can convince one that the cards are evil.

Many people, including children are looking for power or the ability to control others. They also have an innate desire to fill the void in their lives. All are searching for meaning and fulfillment in life. Having God as the center and not us will fulfill the longings we have. God has all power and gives meaning to our lives. The only spirit to look to for help is the Holy Spirit. In fact, we are commanded to walk by the Spirit in Galatians 5:16, "I say then; 'Walk in the Spirit, and you shall not fulfill the lust of the flesh.' " The Holy Spirit can give us power. So many are searching for power in the wrong places.

SIGNS OF A CHILDS INVOLVEMENT IN A CULT

One of the main signs that a young person may be leaning toward a cult is their attire. Their clothing, hair color or style, and make-up may be a sign of inner struggle. Young people are looking for identity and acceptance. If children dress in a particular way they feel accepted by others who also dress this way. By letting them dress in fashion with Satanic symbols is contrary to loving God. The fascination of the symbols can lead one to experimenting to see if they really have power. Children dressed in black, painting their nails black and their faces white, are displaying an obsession with darkness.

Another warning is rock music. The average teenager listens to 10,5000 hours of rock music between the seventh and twelfth grade.[14] Music molds and influences ones behavior because the lyrics are from the pit, by that I mean the songs are inspired by Satan himself. Some of the songs deal with death, sex, drugs, corpses, human sacrifices, Jesus as a deceiver, or the death of God. The music and words settle in their subconscious and before long they begin to act it out. Parents should stay informed about what their children are listening to.

More serious symptoms manifested in children may be a very low self-esteem, disinterest in the spiritual, wrong choice of friends, drug or alcohol abuse, fascination with occult symbols, literature or satanic charms. As they become more involved, they may be interested in knives which are used in satanic sacrifices, obsessed with death or suicide, satanic religious artifacts and bells used in satanic rituals, books, journals, diaries that deal with the occult, and even ritual altars decorated with red, white, or black candles, knives, or even animal bones. By this time they are usually very involved in satanic worship.

Parents need to be aware of any personality changes. They might become very withdrawn, sad, secretive, hostile, angry, abusive, arrogant, loud or show disrespect for authority and their parents. Many times they will get hooked on drugs, sex, and alcohol. They may even speak of death or suicide. Frequently children may become confused or mentally disorientated. Some times they may depict one or more different personalities. The manifestations in their personality are the fruits of darkness, which come from demonic spirits. Once a child has reached this state they will need to be set free from the bondages of

Satan. Romans 8:15 states who we are to be in bondage to, "For you did not receive the spirit of bondage again to fear, but you received the Spirit of adoption by whom we cry out 'Abba, Father.'"

PART 6

Freedom From Cults And Attitude Toward Cults

Chapter XIII

Discernment Of Spirits

In 1 Corinthians 12:10 the Word says, "to another the working of miracles, to another prophecy, to another discerning of spirits, to another different kinds of tongues, to another the interpretation of tongues." Discerning of spirits is very important to prevent us from being deceived or influenced by those involved in cults. The footnote in the *Spirit Filled Bible* defines discerning of spirits as the ability to discern the spirit world, and especially to detect the true source of circumstances or motives of people (p.1737).

Vines Expository of New Testament Words, defines the word discern "diakrisis" as meaning a distinguishing, a clear discrimination, discerning, judging is translated "discerning." If we are to survive the world today, we must have the gift of discerning of spirits. We have not because we ask not. If we ask God for it we shall receive it. We must believe that we have received. This takes faith to believe. God confirms it in His Word in Hebrews 11:6, "But without faith it is impossible to please Him, for he who comes to God must believe that He is, and that He is a rewarder of those who diligently seek Him." We can walk in the gift of discernment.

Just like Satan tempted Jesus, so will the world, the flesh, or the devil tempt us. Every Christian needs to be able to discern if it is their own flesh (1 Corinthians 2:11), the lying spirit of Satan (1 John 4:3,), or if it is the Holy Spirit (1 Corinthians 2:12). This is the discernment of the spirits operating in our lives.

In Rev. Ray Patterson's book, *House Beautiful*, he lists three major points to keep in mind. He says discerning of spirits is:

1. An ability to discern beyond your natural ability.
2. An ability to discern whether various spirits are of God or not.
3. An ability to discern what kind of spirits are causing a particular bondage (p. 76-77).

This gift is needed in the body of Christ and has been neglected in our churches. We are to "Be sober, be vigilant; because your adversary the devil walks about like a roaring lion, seeking whom he may devour" (1 Peter 5:8). A good example of the gift of discernment of the spirits in the New Testament is in Acts 5, Ananias and Sapphira tried to impress the church with their generosity and lied about the money received for the land they sold. Peter discerned that they had lied about the amount of money received. Under the direction of the Holy Spirit, Peter told them they had not lied to man but to God. Ananias dropped dead. Three hours later the same lying spirit in Sapphira caused her to drop dead (Acts 5:1-11). Seeing this power manifested, the people feared God and the church grew daily. This would cause people to get serious with God if it happened today. Personally, I believe we will see those days again.

One day I was walking out of a store and a mother with a two year old child was ahead of me. The child was crying and wanted her mother to carry her. She refused to put her legs down and walk. (Her mother was carrying her out by holding her by the arm). Again she told her daughter to put her legs down and walk. The little girl refused. Under my breath I felt impressed to command the spirit of disobedience to go out of her. The child put her legs down and walked! She also stopped crying. I discerned the spirit of disobedience.

Another time I was taking care of several children while the mothers were in a Bible study. I didn't know the history of any of the children. This particular day I took a seven month-old girl on my lap and was rocking her. I felt impressed to quietly bind generational curses off of her. Immediately she vomited! When her mother came to get her I asked it she had been sick at all that day, she answered, "No, she has been just fine." Apparently the generational curse came out; at least that was my discernment.

If we are not completely sure of which spirit is in control, we would have to try the spirits. In 1 John 4:1 it states, "Beloved, do not believe every spirit, but test the spirits, whether they are of God; because many false prophets have gone out into the world." Through study of the Word, Mary Garrison wrote, *How To Try A Spirit,* realized that she must first bind the strongman, which is the main controlling demon. It says in Matthew 12:29, "Or how can one enter a strongman's house and plunder his goods, unless he first binds the strongman? And then he will plunder his house." She did as the Word said and it worked.

I heard Bob Larson say that he first delivers all the small demons to weaken the strongman. In this way the strongman leaves quicker. There is probably no right or wrong way as they are both addressing the scriptural strongman. Walking in the gift of discernment of spirits and listening to the voice of the Holy Spirit is an important element to free people of demonic influence.

I do not believe a Christian can be possessed. They can

be obsessed which is the domination of ones thoughts or feelings by a persistent idea, image, and desire. They may also be oppressed. Webster says, "obsession is a persistent disturbing preoccupation with an often unreasonable idea causing such a preoccupation" (p.583). An example might be washing ones hands continually. A person will do this thinking they will be washing away the guilt of sin. Webster defines oppression as, "a sense of heaviness or obstruction in the body or mind (p.593)." Webster says that oppression can also be depression. Obsession and oppression can be a spirit or it could also be from a chemical imbalance. The person would need to have blood tests to discern if it is a metabolic disturbance. If it is not metabolic, then the manifestations in the person can be handled as a spiritual problem.

If a person has heaviness and feel weighted down the Bible tell us to put on the garment of praise for a spirit of heaviness (Isaiah 61:3). Satan hates praise as he was cast out of heaven because he wanted to be praised like God. When people sing God's praises the enemy leaves because he cannot stand praise and worship of God.

SALVATION

Because of Satan's pride, God banned him from heaven, and was cast to the earth. In Genesis 3:14-15 God said to the serpent, "Because you have done this, you are cursed more than all cattle, and more than every beast of the field; on your belly you shall go, and you shall eat dust all the days of your life. And I will put enmity between you and the woman, and between your seed and her Seed. He shall bruise your head, and you shall bruise His heel." This scripture is the promise from God that Jesus is Eve's seed through Mary, and shall bruise Satan's head. We know that Satan goes about the earth seeking whom he may devour (1 Peter 5:8). This is exactly what he does to people who have never been saved and made Jesus Lord of their lives. Before a person is saved (born again), they belong to Satan and usually have no inner peace or joy.

The first step in becoming free from demonic activity is to receive salvation. It is a free gift just for the asking. This is verified in Ephesians 2:8, "For by grace you have been saved through faith, and that not of yourselves; it is the gift of God, not of works, lest anyone should boast." When Jesus enters our spirit it is regenerated and we become a new creation. This releases the hold Satan can have on a Christian. Many times people are saved, healed and delivered all at the time of salvation.

The following is an example of why every one needs to be saved. There is a void or emptiness in us that can only be filled by God. This is a story of a young girl searching for the void to be filled and was looking in all the wrong places.

This young girl had been home schooled. Her parents gave her permission to have a pen pal. The pen pal was involved in a cult and influenced the girl with ideas regarding witchcraft. She started to wear black, listen to other kinds of music, and became withdrawn. In her diary were thoughts of death by starvation.

About this same time my husband and I were led to visit her home. Every time I mentioned the name of Jesus, she would jerk her head to the side trying to avoid eye contact. In her eyes I discerned a spirit of death and suicide and she needed help quickly.

Her parents got her into a Christian Boarding School that dealt with such problems. Several weeks later she surrendered to the Lord. This is her story in her own words printed with her permission.

"My life was changed after I met Jesus Christ. Having grown up in a Christian family, I've known about Jesus all my life. I had always accepted, never questioning it wasn't true, until I became older and curious about the things not spoken about in public or family circles. I wanted something different than what I saw in others' lives. I wanted to satisfy the need inside me that I thought no one else had.

My parents saw a change in me as my desires changed-they watched as I started "testing life." I wanted to find out where my boundaries were; I wanted to see how far I could push life and still make it.

Not finding fulfillment in "living just to live" (because without a relationship with Jesus life IS empty). I pursued my curiosities until they had taken over my life. The clothes I wore were black because the music I listened to left me black inside. I thought I was different than everyone else and wanted to make myself as different as I could-confusion was all I knew. My purpose was only about fulfilling my own destructive desires.

My parents tried counselors and anything they hoped would bring healing. They tried letting the state take care of me; sending me to a wilderness program, but nothing filled the void I knew-it might for a little while, but in the end it was always <u>worse</u> than before. At the lowest place of my life they turned from the world's help to God—they brought me to a ministry for teens that opened the door for my salvation.

Determined not to change, I closed my heart to any love and thought I had gone too far for God to save me. I wanted back into "my" world, where I would not have to hear the truth-where truth was whatever I decided it would be. This could not last for long. I had to make a choice-what was real? Was I going to keep fighting God, and live as the servant of hate? My only hope was to look to Jesus. I needed life! I had no life inside. John 14:6 Jesus said, "I am the way, the truth, and the life; no man cometh unto the Father, but by Me." John 3:18, "He that believeth on him is not condemned; but he that believeth not is condemned already, because he hath not believed in the name of the only begotten Son of God."

For whosoever (that means even you) shall call upon the name of the Lord shall be saved. The Bible says that Jesus is coming again: where do you stand before God? In the 16 years of my life I've learned enough to know that the Bible is true, and that Jesus is real. This makes things simple. I need nothing but Him; and am learning to trust. What does Jesus mean to you?"

In her search for God the forces of darkness were drawing this young lady. This is one of the main reasons people enter cults as well as the other reasons I mentioned earlier. Jesus is the sure way here and for hereafter-in eternity. John 3:19-21 says it well, "And this is the condemnation, that the light has come into the world, and men loved darkness rather than light, because their deeds were evil. For everyone practicing evil hates the light and does not come to the light, lest his deeds should be exposed. But he who does the truth comes to the light, that his deeds may be clearly seen, that they have been done in God."

FILLED WITH THE SPIRIT

Additional help to remain free of demonic activity is to be filled with the Holy Spirit. When one receives Jesus in their heart they also receive the Father, Son, and Holy Spirit, as these three are one. We are commanded to "Be filled with the Spirit" in Ephesians 5:18. It is also a baptism of power as stated in Luke 24:29, "Behold I send the Promise of My Father upon you; but tarry in the city of Jerusalem until you are endued with power from high." The more power we have with God the less authority the enemy can have over us.

There is more than one baptism mentioned in the Bible. For example Hebrews 6:2 speaks "of the doctrine of baptisms, of laying on of hands, or resurrection of the dead, and of eternal judgment." When Paul came to Ephesus he said to the Christians, "Did you receive the Holy Spirit when you believed?" So they said to him 'We have not so much as heard whether there is a Holy Spirit.' And he said to them, 'Into what then were you baptized?' So they said 'Into John's baptism.' Then Paul said, 'John indeed baptized with a baptism of repentance, saying to the people that they should believe on Him who would come after Him, that is, on Christ Jesus.' When they heard this, they were baptized in the name of the Lord Jesus. And when Paul laid hands on them, the Holy Spirit came upon them, and they spoke with tongues and prophesied" (Acts 19:2-6). The baptism of the Holy Spirit is an immersion of a relationship with the Holy Spirit. The born again experience is the same as the baptism of repentance of John, and is a baptism into Christ.

If there are two glasses and one is full of water and one has just a little in it, both have water in them. This is an example of the fullness of the Holy Spirit. We can have the Holy Spirit or we can have the fullness of the Holy Spirit. The choice is ours and it can be ours for the asking.

The Holy Spirit will also pour the love of God in our hearts (Romans 5:5). This love can produce praise of God. When we praise God some demons will flee. Satan was praising God before His throne prior to his prideful fall to the earth. He hates praise and worship of God. Frequently demons will leave the captives when they are worshipping God.

DELIVERANCE

What many churches miss today is the command given in Matthew 10:7-8 "And as you go, preach, saying; The kingdom of heaven is at hand. Heal the sick, cleanse the lepers, raise the dead, cast out demons. Freely you have received, freely give." As our society appears to be coming more sinful, there is a greater need for deliverance. By opening the door to sin, it gives the enemy a way of entry into a person. This is why an alcoholic gets worse and worse. When the "spirits fermenti" (alcohol) produces a subliminal state with ones soul (will), the enemy can enter and begin to take over. An alcoholic will be deceived and rationalize another drink. They lie, steal, and hide their bottles. Sometimes they become loud, obnoxious, and fighting. The bondage gets worse and worse as Satan takes more possession of them every time they go on a binge. The same thing happens when a person takes drugs. At this point an alcoholic or anyone who is in spiritual bondage would need deliverance. They may be bound by generational curses or the generational iniquities and inappropriate soul ties. Repentance is needed, then salvation, and the infilling of the Holy Spirit. Sometimes they are so bound they cannot come to Jesus. This is where the one doing the deliverance should check the background of their past history as well as having the Gift of Discerning of the Holy Spirit. The Holy Spirit is our helper and must be totally relied on (John 14:16).

The person or team doing the deliverance must know what they are doing, and know their power and authority they have in Christ. If not, the one being delivered may be caused more emotional trauma by not being completely delivered or filled with greater fear.

Instead of speaking of demons, it is best to refer to them as "enemy spirits." Also the terminology of "spiritual bondage" or "under a spiritual attack" is preferable. Be kind and try not to frighten the person receiving ministry.

It is preferable to have the person receiving the deliverance fill out an identification form. The results of the information received should be prayed over for further discernment. Ask the Holy Spirit for guidance. On the day of deliverance the entire team should have fasted so they are more sensitive to the Holy Spirit, and Jesus said that some demons only come out by prayer and fasting. Matthew 17:19-21 declares, "Then the disciples came to Jesus privately and said, 'Why could we not cast it out?' So Jesus said to them, 'Because of your unbelief; for assuredly, I say to you, if you have faith as a mustard seed, you will say to this mountain, 'Move from here to there,' and it will move; and nothing will be impossible for you.'" 'However, this kind does not go out except by prayer and fasting.'" Jesus confirms it in His Word.

The reason there are several on a team is if one gets tired, another person can take over. God may use different people on the team to reveal different things in order for a person to be delivered. Usually after an hour or two and at the direction of the Holy Spirit, the session should stop and continue another day. It is too tiring for all, and the Holy Spirit knows how much the person being delivered can take in one setting.

The place of deliverance should be in a quiet, private room where there are no distractions. The room should have been anointed and sealed off by the Holy Spirit. Exodus 40:9 says, "And you shall take the anointing oil, and anoint the tabernacle and all that is in it; and you shall hallow it and all its utensils, and it shall be holy." This also prevents the operation of "astral projection" by satanic spirits.

If a man is being delivered men should do the deliverance, or at least have men present in the room. Women should have women present for their deliverance. Women should be encouraged to dress in pants to avoid unnecessary exposure. The person being delivered will sometimes thrash around, scream, gnash their teeth, or crawl like a snake. In this case the demons should be commanded not to use the persons body by putting them through contortions. Sometimes the demons will cause the person to go into a sleep and it gives the appearance that they have been delivered. In this case the person doing the deliverance can command them to come back and pay attention. Frequently the person will keep their eyes tightly closed. Open the eyelids and speak to the demons seen in the eyes so they can no longer hide. Every command to the demons must be made in the name of Jesus. As it says in Philippians 2:10, "that at the name of Jesus every knee should bow, of those in heaven, and of those on earth, and of those under the earth." Ones authority comes from the name and blood of Jesus, and the Word of God.

IDENTIFICATION SHEET

Before a deliverance session, it is helpful to have the person fill out a personal identification sheet. This will help eliminate the length of time necessary at one session. Frequently the one being delivered cannot recall everything at once or they may not even be aware that there was a cultic connection. Any involvement could give the enemy legal right to enter that person. This aids the one setting the captive free to cover all appropriate areas. The following is an example of an identification sheet or questionnaire. It can be used in a self-deliverance.

**Circle the following if you or anyone in
your family has been involved in the following:**

Aetherius Society, Anands Marga Yoga Society, Armstrongism, Ascended Masters Astara, Astrology, Baha'I, Buddhism, Christian Science, Church of Latter Day Saints (Mormonism), Cole-Whitaker, Crowleyism, Da Free John, Enchankar, Esalen Institute, Findhorn Foundation, Free Masonry, Hinduism, Holism, Human Potential Movement, Hare Krishna, Islamism, Jehovah Witness, Ku Klux Klan, Life Training, MaCumba, Manson Cult, Martial Arts, Montessori Mind Sciences, New Age Cults, Rev. Ike, Rosicrucianism, Scientology, Self-Realization Fellowship, Silva Mind Control, Spiritism, Theosophy, Trance Channeling, Transcendental Meditation,UFO'S, Unification

Church, Unitarianism, Unity School of Christianity, Urantia, Vedanta Society, Voodoo, Witchcraft, or any type of Yoga.

**Circle any that you or your family
have been involved in:**

Dungeons and Dragons, Practicing, Fortune-telling, Horoscopes, Séances, Ouija Boards, Out of Body Experiences, Table or Body lifting, Palm Reading, Terra Cards, Mental Telepathy, Charms, Hypnotism, Superstition, Dowsing (divining rod to find water, minerals or underground cables), Crystal balls, Hypnosis, Omens, Monsters, Astral-projection, Star Gazing or Astrology, Necromancy (Communication with the dead), Prognostication (foretelling from signs and symptoms, prophesying without the Holy Spirit), White or black Magic, Enchantments or Channeling.

**Please circle any repetitive tragedies
in your family line:**

Murders, Divorce, Plagues, Diseases, Abortions, Rape, Alcoholism, Drugs, Poverty, Violence or Physical Abuse, Fire, Abandonment, or other _____

Circle any sexual problem that applies:

Adultery, Homosexuality, Incest, Fornication, Molestation, Peeping Tom, Masturbation, Sexual Desires and Sexual Fantasies, Pornography, Oral, Cyber, or Telephone Sex, any Other_____

Circle anything that applies
to your Emotional Profile:

Abandonment: I feel all alone. No one needs me. I have been overlooked. I am not important. I cannot trust anyone. God has forsaken me.

Confusion: I feel indecisive, unable to make up my mind. Confused about everything. Do not know what to do. Wonder if God can help me?

Fear and Death: Something evil is going to happen to me. I do not like heights. I have fear of water, germs, and small closed areas. If I trust someone I will end up getting hurt. Everyone in my family dies of a certain disease or at a specific age, I cannot cope. Even God does not care.

Hopelessness: It will never get better. There is no way out. I have no choice. Feel trapped. Maybe I should just end it. Too overwhelmed. Even God cannot help me.

Rejection: I was a mistake. I should never been born. Nobody likes me. I feel dumb, stupid, and unattractive. I always make a scene or speak out to get attention, and was never liked because_____
I could never be as good as _____
is. I feel worthless and no good. Even God cannot like me. I feel like a failure.

Shame: I didn't want it to happen. It was all my fault. I was a participant. I should have known better. I deserved it. I kept going back. I feel sick, shameful, dirty, and unclean. Maybe I have a disease. I turn everything inward on myself. No one will be able to love me. God will not love me either.

Circle any destructive habits you may have:

Argumentative, addictions to cigarettes, alcohol, drugs of any kind, gambling, videogames or TV, eating disorder, (anorexia, bulimia, or gluttony), stealing, lying, cheating, rage, thinks of self first, envy, jealousy, lack of order in ones life, too talkative, sleeping problems, laziness, strife, greed, foul mouth, rage, always tardy, forgetful, not dependable, inconsistent, lack discipline, negative attitude, likes rock or New Age music, or compelled to excessive computer use.

Circle any spiritual encounters that apply:

Visions (good or bad), night mares especially about snakes, drowning, or bad dreams about many things, hear audible voices, talking back to the voices, have visitations or see angels or demons, have premonitions (good or bad). God is far away.

Describe your relationship with your Mother:

_____

_____

_____

Anything you were told happened while your mother was pregnant with you:

_____

_____

_____

Describe your relationship with your father:

_____

_____

_____

How do you relate with other people?

_____

_____

_____

Do you recall any promises, ungodly pacts, or vows you made?

_____

_____

_____

Can you recall any negative statements ever made about you from any source or words such as "damn you" or "you'll never amount to anything?"

_____

_____

_____

Is there one thing you hoped would not be asked in this questionnaire?

_____

_____

_____

It is important that the person affirms or reaffirms that they are born again and that Jesus is Lord of their life. They should pray a prayer of renouncement of all the cultic activities they have been involved in. For example they may say, "I renounce you Satan and all your works in my life (name the involvements). I command you to go and stay gone in the name of Jesus. I commit my entire body, soul, and spirit to you Jesus. Of my own free will, I chose to serve you completely as Lord of my life."

It is very important that the person begin to walk in the Spirit. They do this by studying the Word. Romans 10:17

tell us that faith comes from hearing the Word of God. The Scriptures on deliverance, protection, and the power in the Name and Blood of Jesus is equally important. Some that could be studied are Psalm 91, Exodus 1:23, Isaiah 54:17, Romans 8:28-39, Luke 10:17, Mark 16:17, John 10:27-29, or Ephesians 2:6; 6:10,13.

A consistent prayer life is essential. In Luke 18:1 we are told that men ought to pray always and not to faint. If praying is important for any Christian, it is doubly important for a captive who has just been set free. Also in Jude 20 it tells us we can be built up in our inner man by praying in the Holy Spirit. When we are so full of the Holy Spirit, there is no room for any demonic activity. The Holy Spirit is our helper and He will assist us so that we do not give place to the Devil (Ephesians 4:27).

When a newly delivered person begins to think back about the cult they were in they can claim to have the mind of Christ (1 Corinthians 2:16), and then begin to praise the blood of Jesus. If it seems strange to claim the blood of Jesus, recall what God says about the blood in the Bible. When Adam and Eve sinned, God killed an animal by shedding its blood. The blood of a perfect animal was slaughtered as an offering to God for our sins (Genesis 3:21). The blood is the only way of atoning for our sins as stated in Leviticus 17:11, "For the life of the flesh is in the blood, and I have given it to you upon the altar to make atonement for your souls; for it is the blood that makes atonement for the soul." This was symbolic of the blood sacrifice of Jesus in the New Testament when he shed His blood for our sins. A prayer they may pray is:

> Jesus I praise you for shedding your blood for me. It is through your blood that I am saved and all my sins are forgiven and I am washed clean by your precious blood. I worship you through the blood

because you have delivered me from the world and Satan's influence. Through your blood I am delivered from death and hell. I praise you for the blood because it has freed me from all sickness and disease over 2000 years ago when you shed your blood for me on Calvary. Thank you for delivering me from the curse. I believe that by your shed blood I am free from all failures and poverty. Through your blood I am thankful for being a member of the kingdom of God, and have the eternal kingdom in me. I worship the Father, Son and Holy Spirit because of the blood. I am a blessed person. Again I praise the blood of Jesus and renounce any pacts made with Satan."

This is a very powerful prayer and one can feel the enemy leave, as he hates the blood of Jesus. Ask Jesus to come in to your heart to be your Lord and Savior. Ask to take away your sins and surrender everything to Him. Make Him Lord of your life. If you have never done this before, it should give you great peace.

I suggest you tell another Christian what you just did to confirm it in your heart. Look for a church to attend that is alive and preaches the Word of God. Read the Bible every day and it would be helpful to get into a Bible Study. Spend time with the Lord by praying and seek to know Him. We cannot know someone if we do not take the time to be with them. He loves you so much He came from heaven just for you. You are important to Him and everyone else that loves the Lord.

BLESSINGS

God tells us to bless those who curse us. There is power in the spoken word. Job 22:28 states "You will also declare a thing, and it will be established for you; so light will shine on your ways." There is power of life and death in the tongue. God spoke everything into existence by His words. His words were creative words. In Genesis 1:28 it says, "Then God blessed them, and God said to them, 'Be fruitful and multiply; fill the earth and subdue it; have dominion over the fish of the sea, over the birds of the air, and over every living thing that moves on the earth.'" God spoke blessings, so we should also speak blessings.

Moses had to put a choice before the Israelites prior to entering Canaan, "I call heaven and earth as witnesses today against you, that I have set before you life and death, blessing and cursing; therefore choose life, that both you and your descendents may live;" (Deuteronomy 30:19). They were to make a choice. God would not make a choice for them. The decision they would make would not only affect them at the present but also for future generations. They could exchange curses for blessings.

Blessings in the Greek according to *Vines,* comes from the word "eulogeo" which means to speak well of, to praise, to celebrate with praise of that which is addressed to God, acknowledging His goodness, with desire for His glory. It also means to invoke blessings upon a person and has the meaning of bounty. Lastly it means to consecrate a thing with solemn prayer, to ask God's blessing on a thing (p.132).

When we bless a person, we are imitating God and using His power setting things in motion. Jesus said greater things we will do that He has done. A positive confession is a good way to begin. Also in Psalm 145:11 states, "They shall speak of the glory of Your kingdom, and talk of Your power." There is power in the spoken word. We are to speak blessings and not curses. Luke 6:28 tell us exactly what we are to do, "Bless those who curse you, and pray for those who spitefully use you." Once we realize that the greater One lives in us, then when we speak, we can accomplish what Jesus did and more. Not because of us but because the anointed One in us is speaking.

All through the Old Testament the Jewish fathers would speak a blessing over their children when they reached puberty. It was a time of special celebration. It was a positive spiritual blessing. Usually everything the father spoke over them came to pass. We know too from the New Testament that the Word is powerful like a double-edge sword (Hebrews 4:12). So in conclusion we have a choice to choose whether we will speak blessings or chose curses. Lets choose blessings!

ATTITUDE TOWARD CULTS

Since we know who our enemy is, it is very important that we know the truth so we will not be deceived. For one to know the truth, we should study the written Word. The Word is Jesus who became flesh for our salvation. He taught us how to live by His own example. He is the way the truth and the life.

Our own attitude should convey the love of Christ. We need not fear being around anyone who is involved in a false religion or a cult. We are to be the light that dispels darkness. Jesus did not come for the righteous, but the sinner who needs Him. We all need to ask ourselves if we know the Bible well enough to confront a person still in darkness, so we can share the Truth with them. It is the Truth that will set the captives free. The Truth shared in love has a powerful and everlasting life effect.

Also our attitude toward those beginning to be involved in a cult should be to warn them of the dangers. Show them in the Word why they are in error. If they are entrenched already, and refuse to acknowledge the truth, then love them and pray for them. If they need deliverance, then seek help for them. We are to set the captives free. If we are not sensitive or mature enough in the Spirit, go with them to someone who is in a deliverance ministry.

Whenever people seek to be enlightened by the force or reach new heights of enlightenment, Satan is there to infiltrate their minds. We are commanded to meditate on the Word of God continuously and have the mind of Christ. As a Christian, enlightenment comes through the power of God. Prayer is the power of God. Praying God's Word and the name of Jesus will bring one to victory because God watches over His Word to fulfill it (Isaiah 55:11). No word of God remains void that God sent it out to accomplish.

The truth is in God's inspired words in the Bible. According to 1 Corinthians 8:6 it states, "Yet for us there is one God the Father, of whom are all things, and we for Him; and one Lord Jesus Christ, through whom are all things, and through whom we live." This proves that the New Age people and others cannot become gods themselves. For example the "I Am All In All" from the I Am Institute of Applied Metaphysics suggests that man is the center of the universe and is self-sufficient. They are obviously deceived. Only the truth will keep them set free.

If man could become God, then one could easily see that there would be no morality, sin, or absolute truth. What ever they think is right is what they chose to believe. This would negate our need for redemption from the original sin of Adam and Eve. Jesus' death was a ransom for this sin.

Cults like to exalt themselves and their leaders. Jesus alone is to be exalted. He is the way, the truth, and the life. No one comes to the Father except through Jesus. God will cast down Satan and he will be bound for a thousand years like the Word says in Revelation 20:1-3, "Then I saw an angel coming down from heaven, having the key to the bottomless pit and a great chain in his hand. He laid hold of the dragon, that serpent of old, who is the Devil and Satan, and bound him for a thousand years; and he cast him into the bottomless pit, and shut him up, and set a seal on him, so that he should deceive the nations no more till the thousand years were finished. But after these things he must be released for a little while." No one wants to follow a looser like that!

After being in a cult, Satan will not easily let them go. Sometimes he will bombard them with wrong thought, confusion or even torment their minds. Until they are completely set free, they could experience astrol projection. Keep yourself and them covered with the blood of Jesus and anoint both with the oil of the Holy Spirit.

Naturally it is important that their mind be renewed through the study of the Word. It is imperative that they attend a church where the Word is preached. Through it all they will experience a peace that only God can give. Like St. Augustine said in the third Century, "My heart is restless until it rests in Thee." What people involved in New Age and in cults are searching for, can only find fulfillment in a relationship with God, the creator of everything and everyone.

PART 7

The Christian's Responsibility Of Aftercare

Chapter XIV

The Christian's Responsibility Of Aftercare

W hen a person comes out of a cult and is saved, they are a new creation in Christ. The individual can still have problems that the church must be aware of. It is believed that it takes from three to eight years for one to adjust to the "Christian" life style.

There are three critical ingredients that affect a newly delivered Cultist. They feel all their roots have been ripped off. No longer is there any identity with the former people and they feel alone. Because of this there is the temptation to go back to their cult family.

The second ingredient is that they no longer have a story. The history of a culture's heritage and the so-called heroes of their previous culture, no longer exists. They recall all the culture practices, doctrines, faith experiences, and love for the previous religion. This is difficult, as they have not established new religious practices.

The third ingredient is one of identity. Their identity confirms ones existence, gives assurance that one has meaning in life. Without self-esteem and positive self-image, they feel like a fish out of water. There is a sense that they are strangers even to themselves and others.

Christians can help by being perceptive. We can let them know that we understand that they gave up everything that was dear to them. Make them feel secure and that we are there for them. Do not put down the cult in front of them as they may feel a loyalty to the cult for a while. Give them a chance to adjust.

A Christian should become informed of the concerns of someone who has just left a cult. An ex-Cultist does not always understand why they feel like they do. An informed Christian or church can help identify their problems and help them work it through. Always be polite. Sometimes specific scriptures will minister to them and help the to maintain spiritual stability.

One may pray for the ex-Cultist by praying for their specific needs. Sometimes their concept of Jesus did not change but their doctrines have. Because of this they need patience and loving reassurance. God will hear their prayer and ours. Proverbs 21:31b clearly states, "But deliverance is of the LORD."

Another important help for a new convert is to be available. They need a shoulder to lean on. Let them know they may call at any time and the door is always open. Always be humble, open, and seek the wisdom of the Holy Spirit in ones dealing with them.

Many ex-Cultists, especially Mormons, vacillate in their convictions. One minute they are convinced that Christianity is the true religion and the next minute they feel Mormonism may have been right. According to Janis Hutchinson, an ex-Mormon, she explains that there are four reasons they do this. They are:

"First, her pride is at stake. As a faithful Mormon, Beth has been trained to boast that her church has special insight into the mysteries of life that others don't have, plus a restored gospel, modern-day prophet, extra-biblical revelation, and visitations from resurrected beings. She can't let go of that kind of uniqueness.

Second, her ego is at stake. She's ashamed to admit she might be wrong about her faith. It's a terrible thing to admit you've been duped—it makes one feel stupid. For her to admit she's been wrongis the same as her admitting she's not able to discern truth from error and she wants to appear spiritually mature to you.

Third, her whole belief system is at stake. In spite of her doubts about Mormonism, she still cherishes her beliefs because of the faith they instill in her. Something deep within her knows how devastating it will be once she acknowledges Mormonism is false.

Fourth, her secure and anxiety-free world is at stake. The cult for many years has been like a mother—succoring, counseling, doing her thinking, protecting, providing for her needs. It's threatening to step out of that world."[15]

This is why we have to go slow with ex-Cultists. Unless we understand them, they will be tempted to go back to the security of a cult. It means we have to have Godly wisdom, understanding, loving kindness, and patience.

Most ex-Mormons have dreams or even nightmares about Mormonism, Joseph Smith, or Brigham Young. They may be plagued with thoughts of them or their teachings during the day as well. One way to overcome that is to do what Psalm 50:15 says, "Call upon Me in the day of trouble; I will deliver you, and you shall glorify Me." By calling on the name of Jesus and speaking it aloud it will help them to believe in their heart. This is confirmed in the Word of God in Romans 10:9-11, "That if you confess with your mouth the Lord Jesus and believe in your heart that God has raised Him from the dead, you will be saved. For with the heart one believes unto righteousness, and with the mouth confession is made unto salvation. For the Scripture says; 'Whoever believes on Him will not be put to shame.' "

When the timing is right, the ex-Mormon or any ex-Cultist should be assisted in renouncing the cultic belief. They need to be specific. For example an ex-Mormon should say that, "I renounce the *Book of Mormon,* any of the writings of Joseph Smith and Brigham Young." All of the literature and books need to be destroyed for the captive to be set free. Until that is done our enemy has a hold. We need to know thy enemy.

Selected Bibliography

A *Frank Exposure of Freemasonry* reprinted from *The Baptist Examiner.* Ashland, KY, Chicago, IL: National Christian Association. No date.

Anderson, Neil T. and Steve Russo. *The Seduction of our Children.* Eugene, OR: Harvest House Publications, 1991.

Ankerberg, John and Craig Branch. *The Thieves Of Innocence.* Eugene, OR: Harvest Publishers, 1993.

Annacondia, Carlos, *Listen To Me Satan* Lake Mary, FL, Creation House, 1998.

Arthur, Kay. *Lord is it Warfare?* Sisters, OR: Multnmomah Publishers, Inc., 1991.

Beck, Hubert. *The Cults.* St. Louis, MO: C.P.H., 1995.

Bottari, Pablo. *Free In Christ.* Lakeland, FL: Creation House, 2000.

Brooke, Tal. *Virtual Gods.* Eugene, OR: Harvest House, 1997.

Brown, Rebecca, M.D. *He Came to Set the Captives Free.* Chino, CA: Chick Publications, (P.O. Box 662, 91710), 1986.

Fact File as featured on the 700 Club, aired June 1, 1999, N152.

Garrison, Mary. *How to Try A Spirit.* New Port Richey, FL: Mary Garrison Ministry, 1989.

Gibson, Noel and Phyl. *Deliver Our Children From The Evil One.* Kent, England TN11OZS, Sovereign World Ltd., 1992.

Greenwald, Gary L..*Seductions Exposed.* Santa Ana, CA: Eagles's Nest Publications, 1989.Gumprecht, Jane, M.D. *New Age Health Care Holy Or Holistic.* Orange, CA.: Promise Publishing Co, 1988.

Hagin, Kenneth. *Ministering to the Oppressed.* Tulsa, OK: Kenneth Hagin Ministries, 1969.

Hayes, Norvel. *Know Your Enemy.* Tulsa, OK: Harrison House, 1990.

Hinn, Benny. *War in the Heavenlies.* Dallas, TX:Heritage Printers and Publishers Inc., 1984.

Horrobin, Peter. *Healing Through Deliverance.* Sovereign World LTD. P.O. Box 777. Tonbridge, Kent TN110ZS, England: Sovereign World LTD, 1994

Hunt, Dave, and T.A. McMahon. *America The Sorcerers New Apprentice.* Eugene, OR: Harvest House Publishers, 1988.

Hutchinson, Janis. *Out Of The Cults And Into The Church.* Grand Rapids, MI: Kegel Resources, 1994.

Ing, Richard. *Spiritual Warfare.* New Kingsington, PA: Whitaker House, 1996.

Jensen, Bernard. MD. Nutritionist. *Iridology Simplified,* Escondido, CA,

Jeremiah, David, C.C. Carlson. *Invasion of Other Gods,* Dallas, London, Vancouver, Melbourne: Word Publishing, 1995.

Justice, Nancy. *Charisma Magazine.* "The Pokemon," Feb. 2000.

Kjos, Berit. *Brave New Schools.* Eugene, OR: Harvest Publishers, 1995.

Your Child And The New Age. USA, Canada, England: Victor Books Division of Press Publications Inc., 1990.

Koch, Kurt. *Christian Counseling and Occultism.* Grand Rapids, MI: Kregel Publications, 1985.

Larson, Bob. *In The Name Of Satan.* Nashville, Atlanta, London, Vancouver: Thomas Nelson Publishers, 1996.

Larson's New Book on Cults. Wheaton, IL: Tyndale House Publishers Inc. Revised, 1998.

Dead Air. Nashville, TN: Thomas Nelson Publishers, 1991.

Larson's Book of Spiritual Warfare. Nashville, TN: Thomas Nelson Publishers, 1999.

UFO's and the Alien Agenda. Nashville, TN: Thomas Nelson Publishers,

MacGregor, Lori. *Coping With Cults.* Eugene, OR: Harvest House Publishers, 1992.

MacNutt, Francis. *Deliverance from Evil Spirits.* Grand Rapids, MI: Chosen Books. 1996.

Marrs, Tex. *New Age Cults and Religions.* Austin, TX: Living Truth Ministries, 1996.

Marrs, Wanda. *New Age Lies to Women.* Austin, TX: Living Truth Publishers, 1989.

Martin, Walter. *The Kingdom of the Cults.* Minneapolis, MN: Bethany House Publishers, 1998.

The New Age Cult. Minneapolis, MN: Bethany House Publishers, 1989.

McDowell, Josh, and Don Stewart. *Handbook of Today's Religions.* Nashville, Atlanta, London, Vancouver: Thomas Nelson Publishers, 1983.

Michaelsen, Johanna. *Like Lambs to the Slaughter.* Eugene, R: Harvest House,1989.

Miller, Elliot. *A Crash Course on the New Age Movement.* Grand Rapids, MI: Baker Book House, 1989.

Packer, J. I. And M.C. Tenney. *Illustrated Manners and Customs of the Bible.* Nashville, TN: Thomas Nelson Publishers, 1980.

Patterson, Rev. Ray. *House Beautiful*. New Willington, PA: Son-Rise Publications and Distribution Co., 1986.

Phillips, Phil. *Saturday Morning Mind Control*. Nashville, TN: Thomas Nelson Publishers, 1991. *Turmoil in the Toybox*. Lancaster, PA: Starburst Publishers, 1986.

Phillips, Phil and Joan Hake Robie. *Halloween and Satanism*. Lancaster, PA: Starburst Publishers, 1987.

Pittman, Howard. *Demons an Eyewitness Account*, P. O. Box 107, Foxworth, MS: Howard Pittman Ministries, 1980.

Prince, Derek. *Spiritual Warfare*. Springdale, PA: Whitaker House, 1987. *They Shall Expel Demons*. Grand Rapids, MI: Baker Book House Company 1999.

Reisser, Paul C. and Teri K. and John Weldon. *New Age Medicine*. Downers Grove, IL: Inter Varsity Press, 1987.

Robertson, Judy. *No Regrets How I Found My Way Out of Mormonism*. Light and Life, Communications, 1999.

Sipe, Onjya. *Devils Dropout*. Milford, MI: Matt Media, 1976, *Spirit Filled Bible King James Version*. Nashville, TN.: Thomas Nelson Publishers, Inc., 1991.

Stratford, Lauren. *Satan's Underground*. Eugene, OR: Harvest House, 1988.

Strong, James L.L.D., S.T.D.. *Abingdons Strongs Exhaustive Concordance of the The New Strong's Complete Dictionary of Bible Words*. Nashville, T.:

Thomas Nelson Publishers, 1996.

The New Age Movement, Published by People's Gospel Hour, 5.

Vick, Paul. *Association to Rescue Kids Report.* 8103 Shiloh Ct., Austin, TX: Living Truth Ministries.

Vines, W.E. *An Expository of O.T. Words.* Old Tappan, N.J.: Fleming H. Revell CO, 1966.
Wagner, Doris M. *How To Cast Out Demons.* Ventura, CA: Renew Books, A Division of Gospel Light, 2000.

Webster's Family Dictionary. Toronto, London, Sydney, Auckland: Random House, Inc. 1998.

Webster's Seventh New Collegiate Dictionary. Springfield, MA: G. & C. Merriam Co. 1965.

Welcome. http://user.aol/tstec/hmpage/+sintro.htm: The Theosophical Society *Pasadena, California Internet World Wide Web Page, 1997.*

What is the Theosophical Society http://w.w.w.theosoph cal.org: Theosophical Society Internet Web site, 1997.

Endnotes

[1] Tex Marrs, *New Age Cults and Religions,* 255.

[2] Jane Gumprecht, MD, *New Age Health Care Holy or Holistic,*ii.iii

[3] Fact File as featured on the *700 Club,* aired June 1st, 1999, N152.

[4] Bob Larson, *UFO's and the Alien Agenda, 93.*

[5] Ibid., 131

[6] Bob Larson, *UFO's and the Alien Agenda,* 202, 203.

[7] *Welcome,* http://user. aol/tstec/hmpage/+sintro.him: The Theosophical Society Pasadena, California Internet World Wide Web Page, 1997.

[8] *What is the Theosophical Society* http://www.theosophical Org: Theosophical Society Internet Web site, 1997

[9] Bob Larson, *New Book of Cults,* 110

[10] Josh McDowell and Don Stewart, *Handbook of Today's Religions,* 342.

[11] Tex Marrs, *New Age Cults and Religions,* 255.

[12] *The New Age Movement,* Published by People's Hour, 5.

[13] Bernard Jensen, D.C., Nutritionist, I*ridology Simplified, 2.*

[14] Neil Anderson and Steve Russo, *The Seductions of Our Children,* 90.

[15] Janis Hutchison, *Out of the Cults and Into the Church,* 174.

Printed in the United States
1353500001B/142-366